PROTECTING THE SHADOW

A Year Inside The Adult Protective Services

by Paul D. Buchanan

Branden Books, Boston

D1160789

Library of Congress Cataloging-in-Publication Data

Buchanan, Paul D., 1958-
  Protecting the shadow : a year inside an adult protective services /
by Paul D. Buchanan.
      p. cm.
   ISBN 978-0-8283-2205-8 (pbk. : alk. paper)
   1. Abused elderly--Services for--United States. 2. Older people--
Abuse of--United States. I. Title.
   HV1461.B82 2010
   362.6--dc22
                        2010044868

Branden Books, Boston
PO Box 812094 Wellesley MA 02482
www.brandenbooks.com

Chapter 1
JANUARY

Two Cedarwood City police cruisers rolled up along the curb outside the house at 233 Tower Street, on a crisp, wintry Tuesday morning in the city's poorer central section. A tall, blonde-haired woman in her forties, dressed in a gray overcoat, stood beside a male uniformed officer. The two reviewed documents on the clipboard in the woman's hand. Another woman – dressed in a blue pants suit, with her gray streaked brown hair pulled back in a bun – waited on the walkway in front of the dilapidated gray two-bedroom house. A young man in a blue wind breaker and baseball-style cap – with the yellow letters "C.F.D." for Cedarwood City Fire Department – hovered about the west side of the house, studying the debilitated structure with both his eyes and his hands. Across the street, a small enclave of neighbors gathered to exchange theories about the ensuing activities.

The paint on the old house peeled and crumbled as the blue clad gentleman ran his fingers along the west wall, which had apparently been subjected to years of rain and sun with little protection. Crabgrass and dandelions overwhelmed the dusty front yard, along with old soaked newspapers, crumpled discarded soft drink cups, and shredded scraps of cloth and paper. The cracked and misshapen walkway reached up to a dilapidated wooden porch. A screen door – its rusting, aluminum frame pulling away from the doorway – rested upon the porch, dangling precariously from a single hinge. A bushy ivy vine meandered its way up the east wall beyond the doorway, enveloping the first window pane, broken and dark. Tiles on the roof flapped in the breeze, as leaves and stems from the nearby tree choked the battered rain gutters dangling from the roof.

This rumbling backdrop greeted Patrick Francis Brennan as he stepped from his government-issue, snow white Ford Taurus. A thirty-five year old social worker with Cedarwood (County) Adult Protective Services – known as APS – Brennan wore his mandatory county I.D. badge on his typical ensemble, a short sleeve polo shirt, which matched well with his pants, dark hair, and stubble on his chin. On chilly days such as this, he wore a pullover sweater. A cellular phone clipped to his belt, he carried whatever documentation or information he might need for such a home visit. Rose Enamoto from the Japanese American Citizens Alliance (JACA) had called Brennan on the APS Intake Hotline. She hoped to enlist his intervention with an elderly woman named Lillian Hirose. Weeks ago the fire department had scheduled an eviction of Mrs. Hirose from her house, when they would post the structure as unsafe for human habitation. Despite the efforts of the JACA, Mrs. Hirose had yet to make any arrangements to stay elsewhere. Enamoto hoped Brennan could convince Mrs. Hirose to leave her premises peacefully, before the scene grew any uglier.

"Hey Rose," Brennan called in his distinctive Dublin-born brogue, puffs of steam emerging from his lips against the cool air.

"Hi, Patrick", Rose called, extending her hand. "Thanks for coming."

"Sure. What's the situation?"

"Well", she responded. "Lillian Hirose has been active with the Association for years, and comes to lunch at the senior center almost every day. She reportedly shops for herself, and seems to be able to provide for all her needs. But a neighbor called the fire department and code enforcement several weeks ago, reporting a horrible smell coming from the house, and garbage piled in the back yard. One thing led to another. She was given a thirty day notice seven weeks ago, and she still hasn't shown any sign of being able to move out. Now they're going to post it."

"What's in the backyard?" Brennan asked.

"Garbage, mostly…piles of leaves and twigs, overgrown weeds, and cages", Enamoto replied. "She's an animal lover; cats, rabbits, hamsters. Animal control should be here soon…"

Just then, the blonde woman who had been talking to the uniformed officer eased over, sticking her hand out and saying, "Nina Hilbert, Cedarwood City Code Enforcement."

Brennan shook her hand. "Patrick Brennan, Adult Protective Services."

"Good," replied Hilbert, taking over the conversation, something she seemed quite accustomed to doing. "The man in the blue wind breaker is an inspector with the fire department. He agrees with me that the house has to be posted."

"That bad, huh?" queried Brennan

"Yeah," Hilbert continued, "there's garbage everywhere, the backyard is a fire hazard, and a health hazard for the animals. The plumbing doesn't work, there's no running water, and the stove is broken. Even if could work, it's covered in garbage. Electric wiring's exposed, and there is structural damage in the walls. You can see…" she said, pointing toward the ivy "…how the foliage is growing into the framework of the house."

"So, where's Mrs. Hirose?" Brennan asked.

"Inside. Officer Matthews is trying to get her to come out, but so far she won't. She was hoping maybe you could help."

"I'll do my best," said Brennan. "Let's go in…"

Brennan followed Hilbert to the front porch. Enamoto trailed behind, as if reluctant to actually enter the dwelling. Hilbert carefully leaned the screen door against the wall, and pushed at the creaking front door. The door opened about a third of the way before something blocked its way. As Brennan followed Hilbert in, he became immediately engulfed in the hot, humid aroma of wet newspapers, piled garbage, rotting food, and human waste – all combined in an aroma so powerful it stung his eyes.

"Whoa…!" he gasped, as he stepped past the pantry into the kitchen.

"Latex gloves..?" Hilbert offered. She seemed to have acclimated to the smell.

"Thanks," Brennan nodded, grabbing a small plastic packet from the code enforcement officer. Pulling the gloves over his fingers, he took a moment to look up, and assess the enormity of the mess before him.

Soaked, moldy newspapers and dry, fading newspapers mixed in great columns stacked throughout the kitchen. The color of the kitchen tile could not immediately be discerned, as mud and paper bags and boxes covered the floor wherever the newspapers did not.

Wrapping paper, empty cans, milk cartons, candy wrappers, electric bills, various articles of clothing blanketed the floor, the chairs, the kitchen table, and the shelves. Stacks of canned goods, cake mix boxes, cereal containers, and cracker cartons spilled all over the kitchen counters, cascading onto the floor in great heaps. The refrigerator – the door of which hung ajar – bulged with moldy fruits, brown vegetables, purple meats, plus bowls and Tupperware containing "God knows what." A grayish liquid dripped from the refrigerator door and walls. The refrigerator smelled so disgusting; it could actually be detected above the stench of the rest of the house.

Legions of flies hovered and alighted above the mess. Under the debris, sounds of rustling – no doubt caused by rodents of untold genus – scampered about on the bottom level of the trash. Brennan stepped forward, careful to avoid the tall, plastic buckets filled with brownish-yellowish liquid. He recalled Hilbert's claim that the plumbing did not work in the house, and suddenly realized the repulsive purpose of the buckets. Flies lingered above the bucket's squalid rims.

"Gwen?" Hilbert called.

"In here," a hoarse female voice called from beyond the kitchen door, across the room. Hilbert and Brennan crossed the floor to find a tall, husky female officer at the doorway leading to the back bedroom. Further inside the bedroom stood a short, frail-looking, elderly woman, clinging to the pink shawl wrapped around her dingy, unwashed housecoat. She seemed to be searching frantically through the piles of clothing and papers covering the bed, dresser, desk, and floor. Brennan assumed this woman was Lillian Hirose.

"Are you Mr. Brennan?" the officer asked.

"Patrick Brennan," he said. "I think we've spoken on the phone before, Officer."

"Oh yeah, sure," she said, "I'm Gwen Matthews. I'd figure we'd meet sooner or later."

"Is this Mrs. Hirose?" Brennan asked.

"Yep...as you can see, we're having a little trouble gettin' her outa here. She keeps thinking of things she wants to take with her, but then she can't find what she thought of. She's lookin' for her keys now. She seems pretty alert, and she's supposed to have money, but somehow..." She glanced around the disaster before them. "I don't want to have to call an ambulance for her, but I ain't waitin' much longer."

"A pack rat," Brennan mumbled to himself. Brennan approached Hirose, who continued to search through piles of letters and clothing. "Good mornin', Mrs. Hirose. My name is Patrick. I'm a social worker from the county."

"Irish?"

"Yes, ma'am," Brennan answered apprehensively.

She looked up at Brennan, speaking in a voice which was surprisingly clear and oriented. "I'm looking for my keys," she said. "I had them when I went shopping this morning, and now I can't find them."

"Do y' know why I'm here, Mrs. Hirose?" Brennan asked.

"They want me to leave my house," she said with a frown. "I don't want to leave."

"I know y' don't", responded Brennan. "But it's not safe for you t' stay here. The fire department says this house has to be closed, and you're gonna have t' find another place to live."

"But where am I supposed to go?"

"Don't y' have family, or friends you can stay with, at least until somethin' more permanent can be arranged?"

"I have family in Corning, but I don't want to bother them."

"Well, Mrs. Hirose, you're gonna have t' do somethin', even if we have to put you up in a motel, but you can't stay here."

"But I don't want to stay in a motel. Why can't you just leave me alone?

"Because y' can't live here anymore. If y' don't come out. I'll have to call for the ambulance, and then they'll carry y' out."

Hirose stopped to consider the matter, and then pursued another tactic. "But I need my keys...and my wallet...and my checkbook. I can't leave yet..."

Matthews, who was now behind Hirose, suddenly held up a jingling ring of keys in her dark hand. "Here they are," she said. "And here's your purse, with your wallet and checkbook. Here, Patrick…" she said, tossing him the purse. "Why don't you take these?"

Nodding in acknowledgement of the officer's idea, Brennan caught the purse.

"Hey! My keys! My purse..!" Hirose called.

"C'mon, Mrs. Hirose", Brennan beckoned, walking slowly back through the kitchen. He dangled the purse like a bag full of carrots. "Come outside with me, then I'll give you your things, and we can talk about where you'll stay tonight."

"You can't do that!" Hirose squawked. "I have my rights. This is like World War II all over again, you fascists!" But slowly, reluctantly, the elderly woman followed Brennan across the kitchen, and out the front door. She hemmed and hawed, stopping to examine items along the way, and complaining the whole time. But finally, Patrick Brennan walked out the front door and down the steps, followed by Mrs. Hirose, and then Hilbert and Officer Matthews. Brennan breathed deeply, savoring the fresh air of outdoors.

One of the neighbors brought over a couple of chairs, on which Brennan and Mrs. Hirose could sit. Animal control arrived, meanwhile, carrying cages to the back yard of Mrs. Hirose's house. Brennan gave the old woman a few minutes to gather her breath. Hirose seemed calm if nonplused about the whole occasion.

As Mrs. Hirose sat on the plastic lawn chair, Brennan took the opportunity to study her more carefully. Multiple stains tarnished the house coast she wore; it had obviously not seen a washing machine in many months. Her hair appeared unkempt and uncombed, pulled back tightly behind her head. Mrs. Hirose sat quietly, staring somewhat unfocused straight ahead. She blinked several times while Brennan waited; the social worker guessed she had marked visual impairments.

Despite her confusion, Hirose could still provide all the vital information he needed: her date of birth, her social security number. She gave the current date, her address, the time of day, the amount of her monthly social security check. She told him she had grown up in Sacramento, California, and indeed experienced the shame of the interrment of Japanese-Americans during World War II. She and her husband moved to Cedarwood City and bought the house twenty-three years prior. He died fifteen years afterward.

When Brennan asked how the house had come to such a state, she said, "I don't know. I've tried to clean it up before, but it was too much for me to do. My back makes it hard for me to lift things."

"But how do you eat?" Brennan asked. "How do you get food for yourself?"

"I buy bottled water from the store. I buy sandwiches, and go to the senior center for lunch. I manage okay."

As Brennan continued his interview, he became increasingly relieved that he and Officer Matthews succeeded in luring the woman out of the house. "This woman doesn't need a hospital," he said, "she only needs someone to help her."

Mrs. Hirose resembled the many "pack rats" Brennan had seen over the years. Most of them had been born during the Depression, and had the value of money and the thrift of spending ingrained in them at an early age. They usually had money, often a substantial amount. Most of them seemed to function adequately in the community; they appeared basically alert and oriented, able to provide their own food, clothing, and shelter. They displayed no psychosis, or even classic dementia. These people simply could not manage to keep their houses in order, and they refused to spend the money to allow anyone else to do it.

When the pack rats attempted to clean, their frugal nature would not allow them to throw anything out. Convinced everything they owned – no matter how old or beat up – might be of value some day, they could not bear to part with anything. As they aged, they lost the physical ability to undertake what had expended into an insurmountable struggle. Normally, their families seemed powerless to help them, since the pack rats would not allow them to throw anything out either. Sometimes these individuals lived in squalor for years, unnoticed by the rest of the community. Then something – an accident, an illness, a report from a neighbor – breaks the silence, and brings them to the attention of the authorities. Inevitably, someone calls Adult Protective Services.

"Well, what are y' gonna do now?" asked Brennan

"I don't know," Hirose shrugged, pulling her shawl more tightly around her shoulders.

"You said in the house you had family in Corning," Brennan reminded her. "Do y' have an address or phone number for them?"

Hirose hesitated for a moment, as if trying to visualize something, and then peered into her tattered purse. She fished her hand into it for a moment, and then pulled out a green address book with a rubber band around it. She opened it and tried to read it, but she squinted harder, unable to focus her eyes on the handwriting.

"Here", offered Brennan, "let me help you."

Brennan paged through the booklet, until he found the names "Joe, Nancy, Skip Hirose." There was an address and phone number beside them.

"Who is Skip?" Brennan asked.

"He's my nephew or something," said Hirose. "He lives at home, with my son and daughter-in-law."

"How old is he?"

"Oh, I think in his thirties. He's between jobs, I think."

Brennan excused himself for a moment, and stepped away to use his cell phone. The bell at the Hirose home rang several times, until finally the gruff voice of a young man answered. He identified himself as Skip Hirose. When Brennan explained to him the situation, Slip hesitated for a moment, and then said, "Well, we don't see her that much. We're only distant cousins. I think my dad once tried to help her clean the place up several years ago, but it didn't work too well. She couldn't decide what to throw out."

Well, can y' come get her, and let her stay with you for a while? We'll have a social worker come out and work with all of you to find her a long term place to live. But for now, she has no where else to go, and she can't decide what to do."

Skip paused again, apparently weighing the inconvenience of the situation.

"Look, Mr. Hirose," said Brennan, "I don't think it's safe for your grandmother to be in a strange motel by herself. If she has no where else to go, we might have to take her to the county hospital against her will. I'd hate to subject her to that, but I don't see any alternative."

Skip paused a little longer, but apparently his guilt overcame his annoyance – just as Brennan hoped. "I'll be there as soon as I can" Skip sighed.

"Thanks, Mr. Hirose. I'll wait here until you get here."

Brennan hung up the phone. "Phew" he whispered, "that was close."

Brennan returned to Mrs. Hirose's side, engaging in comforting small talk until her relative arrived. Meanwhile, a few neighbors wandered by, offering consolation and sympathetic smiles to the longtime neighbor.

Nearly thirty minutes passed before a maraschino cherry red Mazda pulled up in front of Mrs. Hirose's house. Out of the driver's seat stepped a short, stocky man, with a small black goatee on his chin, and glasses around his eyes. He introduced himself as Skip, here to pick up his older cousin.

"This case will be referred to another social worker…"Brennan reminded Skip, "…who will be in touch with you and your family in a few days, and will work with you to make a permanent arrangement for her"

"Okay," Skip replied, somewhat barren of affect.

Brennan helped Hirose to her feet and into Skip's sports car. She smiled what might be identified as a smile of relief. "Thank you, young man," she said.

As the Mazda sped away, Matthews turned to Brennan and said, "I'm glad you were here, Patrick!"

"Thanks, Gwen," Brennan replied, "good work."

"Thanks, Patrick," said Enamoto, smiling with relief. "That was a sticky one for a while."

"Sure, Rose. We'll take good care of her."

On the following cloudy Wednesday morning, ten miles to the south of Cedarwood City in the town of Richland, two dozen men and women sat around a conference table in the multipurpose room at the Green Oaks Community Center in Richland. Community Center director Jane Kimure called the meeting to order.

"Welcome to the South County Providers Information and Referral Forum," the plump, dark-haired woman announced. "For those of you who have not attended before, this quarterly meeting provides human service providers in the southern end of Cedarwood County an opportunity to network, and to share information about their programs, in hopes of providing better service to our clients."

"Today, our speaker is Donna Briar, intake social worker with the Adult Protective Services unit of Adult Services, a division of Cedarwood County Health Department. Donna has been with the county for eleven years, first working in the long term care division, and now on the Intake hotline for Adult Services. Before coming to the county, Donna worked for seven years as a case manager for Arbor Center, which provides services and training for developmentally disabled adults. Today Donna will be telling us about Cedarwood Adult Protective Services, the work the unit does, and how it might affect our clients."

"Thank you," said an engaging, forty-ish, blonde-haired woman. Stylish and sophisticated, Briar regularly dressed elegantly, this day in a smart purple dress with matching handmade earrings and broach. Products of her own hands, her jewelry anchored a lucrative craft business Briar maintained outside the Adult Services office. Over the years, Briar had attracted a loyal customer base at fairs and sidewalk shows through the region, and she regularly donated her jewelry for various Adult Services functions.

Although standing only five-feet, one inches tall, what Donna Rebecca Briar lacked in stature she made up for in determination and professionalism. Despite the distractions that her second career might bring, Briar remained a tremendous professional. She excelled at handling the hotline, deft at assessing calls and screening referrals, accumulating a vast knowledge of community resources and system information. She specialized in helping callers figure out exactly what they wanted, and the easiest way to obtain it.

"Before I talk about APS itself," she said, "I wanted to present some information about Cedarwood County…"

"As you may know, Cedarwood County extends twenty-seven miles north to south, and fifteen miles east to west, split down the middle by a small range of hills. The east side of the hills is primarily mid-to-upper-class suburbia, with a scattering of high tech developers to the south, and manufacturing and construction industries to the north. The vast majority of residents commute to larger cities beyond the county lines to the north and south, while the many others work in service, government, and retail positions up and down the county.

"Western Cedarwood County is rural, with a vast landscape of farms and ranches spread along the southern two thirds of the western half. Many of the homes on the west side are isolated from one another by acres – and even miles – of agricultural fields and deciduous forests, and the entire area – which is primarily unincorporated – is regularly patrolled by only two Cedarwood County sheriff's deputies. Thus, the engagements and activities undertaken by western Cedarwood residents are vast, varied, and largely undetected.

"In all, nineteen separate cities – ranging in population between 80,000 and 10,000 – plus several hundred square miles of unincorporated area combine to make up Cedarwood County.

"Cedarwood County includes some of the wealthiest communities in the United States, including Huntington in the east central, Woodacre and Ashland to the southeast, and Preston Wood along the southern hills on the east side. The wealth comes from old conservative money, supported by old, conservative ideas. Issues such a homelessness, elder abuse, drug addiction, and disabled veterans do not normally concern much of the population – or, more accurately, they don't like to talk about it.

Alongside the mansions and Mercedes, however, reside pockets of some of the poorest, most socially plagued communities in the state. Rogers Park, in the far southeast corner of the county, is a small town of 32,000 individuals made up for the most part of hard-working, lower middle class residents. But a substantial community of alcoholics, drug dealers, and criminals reside within its limits. Two years ago, Rogers Park claimed the highest per capita homicide rate in the country. Located across the freeway from a prestigious university town within the jurisdiction of the county to the south, Rogers Park residents are constantly reminded of the wealth and opportunities most of them will dream of, but few will ever attain.

"Over the years, Rogers Park had become something of a laboratory of from county and nonprofit social and health services programs: well baby programs, teen mother housing, youth drug diversion, etc. Unfortunately, these programs would often get pilot funding, stir up a lot of hope and promises, and then run out of funding within a year or so. Little wonder may residents of Rogers Park have become resentful and mistrustful of any program offering to "help them help themselves."

"Other poorer cities within the county included northeast Dalton City; the unincorporated section of Richland; and the northeast region of Cedarwood City. All these communities included a substantial multicultural mix of middle and lower-middle class residents, some of whom are undocumented immigrants. Others include the disabled, the disenfranchised, the disenchanted, and the highly disappointed with a system into which they paid money for a good portion of their lives, and then counted on when they became sick, injured, elderly, or unemployed."

The county population includes one of the highest percentages of people 65 and older in the country. Many of them are wealthy individuals, with plenty of assets and property to see them through their old age. These residents provide much of the tax base and political motivation for programs such as APS. But a substantial portion of these elderly residents barely make ends meet on their social security or disability payments. With no rent control practiced in the county – the developers who control much of the political will apparently would not hear of it – many of the poor elderly have no where else to go. Figures of 80% of income going to rent are not unknown. Adding the cost of medical care , prescriptions, and in-home help, many of the poor elderly simply do not have enough resources to cope.

"When the lack of resources places these individuals at risk of their health and safety; when elderly or disabled adults are physically abused or neglected by their caregivers; when rich or poor are fiscally swindled by greedy friends, or relatives, then Cedarwood Adult Protective Services is called."

At the same time the South County Information and Referral Forum commenced in Richland, a tall woman with shoulder-length hair and a pretty face with Polynesian features drove out to the Shady Grove apartments in the town of Baldwyn, to the south. She responded to a APS referral concerning one of the residents. Public Health Nurse Rhonda Louisa Pagan had recently joined the APS unit after serving several years as an emergency room triage nurse for a hospital in Los Angeles, California. Despite her rookie status, she had already impressed the Unit with her courage and her professionalism, no doubt honed through stressful hours at the ER.

The Shady Grove numbered among several apartment complexes in Cedarwood County offering some subsidized housing units for senior residents. Through grants from the local Housing Authority office, these complexes offered studio and one-bedroom apartments for below-market prices. Many of the complexes included meal service in the price. Unfortunately, the demand for these units far exceeded the supply. Shady Grove – like all the others – claiming a waiting list several months long.

Although a Section 8 Housing Certificate program officially existed in the county, its waiting list numbered even greater than those of the subsidized units. In the Section 8 Program, these residents possessing a certificate could use in any apartment complex accepting it, so they were not confined to only a certain number of complexes. Unfortunately, the minuscule number of available certificates left persons on the waiting list five years or more.

Because of the large number of infirmed elderly persons residing in Shady Grove, Cedarwood County Department of Health decided it would be clever to assign a retired part-time nurse to see to the needs of the residents. Unfortunately, because this nurse worked only eight hours per week, she normally had time to only uncover the problems – rather than actually resolve any of them. The more rocks the nurse looked under, the more it became evident Shady Grove serve not simply as an independent housing complex, but instead as a quasi-residential care home – without the staff to adequately serve the residents. The only tenable result of the ill-advised experiment – an increase of referrals to the APS nurse – pleased Rhonda Pagan not a bit.

The resident which the on-site nurse – named Betty Major – referred was an 86-year-old recluse named Leona Pendleton. Pendleton had lived at Shady Grove for many years, and had always been regarded as a loner and an eccentric. She had a habit of collecting items; she seemed to spend a lot of time in her room, coming out only for meals or undefined sojourns into the neighborhood. She had a way of befriending stray cats and birds –neither of which were allowed in the complex. Major often found Pendleton dressed in a strange, disheveled conglomeration of scarves, dresses, pants, and overcoats. She mumbled to herself. But she always managed to get her rent in on time; she never actually harmed anyone, and she always seemed to be physically fit.

But over the last few weeks, Major noticed a change. Pendleton showed signs of illness, and spent a lot more time in her room. Eventually, she requested all of her meals in her room, due to her illness. When Major tried to talk with her or examine her, she would refuse. Pendleton would claim to have recently been – or to soon be going to her doctor, but Major felt certain she had not. Most alarming, Major noticed Pendleton wearing a plain colored scarf around her head. Major claimed she had once seen an open, weeping wound under the scarf but, again, Pendleton forbade examination, and seemed to do nothing to manage it. She would not even say how she injured herself. On top of it all, Pendleton grew more argumentative with fellow residents. Her apartment became increasingly cluttered and unkempt; a cleaning woman once reported bags and boxes occupying Pendleton's shower stall, indicating she had not bathed in many weeks.

Shady Grove stood eleven stories tall on the southeast corner of Midtown Park, in the center of downtown Baldwyn. Pagan left her red Toyota Corolla parked on the street, at the edge of the park grounds and the Shady Grove parking lot. An athletic and avid hiker, Pagan always strode with strength and energy gained in years of backpacking. She briskly walked through the front door, and rode the elevator up to the third floor. Finding room 314, she knocked vigorously upon the door. Hearing no response, Pagan knocked again, rang the doorbell, and called out, "Mrs. Pendleton?"

"What d'ya want?' called a raspy, agitated voice from inside.

"I'm a nurse, Mrs. Pendleton," Pagan called. "I was told you were sick, and I've come to see how you're doing."

"You can't come in," Pendleton called, obviously irritated. "I can't talk to you now. I'm sick."

"I know you're sick. That's why I'm here." said Pagan. "Maybe I can help you."

"I'm seeing my doctor on Friday," Pendleton shouted.

"Who's your doctor?" Pagan asked.

"Dr. White, of course," shouted Pendleton, whose voice seemed to be growing closer to the door. "Don't you think I know my own doctor?"

"When did you make the appointment?"

"Ummm…a few days ago...why are you asking me so many questions?"

"I spoke to Dr. White yesterday, Mr. Pendleton. He said he hasn't heard from you in four years. He's very concerned about you."

"Yeah…well, I'll make an appointment tomorrow."

"Why don't you let me in, and maybe I can help you now."

"No, I don't want you here. Now go away, and leave me alone!"

"But…"

"Just go away."

With no authority or reason – at this point – to force her way in, Pagan had no choice but to withdraw. Without seeing her or speaking with her at length, Pagan could not determine her current medical or cognitive condition.

Pagan stopped at Betty Major's unoccupied office, and left a note.

Dear Betty:

Tried to see Mrs. Pendleton today; she would not let me in. At the moment, I have no way of knowing how serious her condition is.

Please continue to monitor her as well as you can, and call me if you believe the situation is reaching a critical point.

Thanks,

Rhonda Pagan, PHN

While Rhonda Pagan slipped the note under the phone, Donna Briar continued her presentation in Richland.

"Now, Adult Protective Services is one of four separate programs under the auspices of Adult Services in Cedarwood County. The other three include:

One: The Public Guardian, which investigates and manages probate conservatorship cases for individuals who have been declared by Superior Court to no longer possess the capacity – physical and/or cognitive – to manage their lives, due to physical, or organic deterioration and disability

Two: Long Term Case management, which provides social workers who – on a continuing basis – help individuals maintain necessary resources and services to avoid conservatorship or institutionalization. It also includes a special unit for AIDS Case Management, providing services for individuals with the HIV virus.

"Three: In-Home Services (IHS), a program for low-income residents which provides Medicaid recipients the money and in-home assistance to remain in their homes. The services include finding care-givers who can cook, clean, provide personal and hygienic care.

"Adult Protective Services is located in the Big Room – as we call it – in the southwest corner of the Department of Health. The Public Guardian is located in the east third of the room; Long Term Case Management resides in the middle third; APS is situated in the west third. IHS is located in a separate room, north of the Big Room.

The nerve center of APS is a quadrangle of desks and cubicles in the southwest corner of the Big Room, where the Intake Hotline is stationed. We call this area "The Bullpen" as it becomes the center for bull sessions during quiet times. It also serves as the entry point for doctors, nurses, lawyers, home health aids, politicians, neighbors, as well as clients, who require help from APS, or any other program in Adult Services. Intake staff take referrals, provide consultation, and offer information and referral. Social workers, deputy public guardians, and nurses – not only from APS but throughout the Adult Services Division – regularly visit the Bullpen to consult on cases. Between myself and the two other Intake social workers, there are nearly fifty years of social work experience available.

A tall, African-American woman with short hair raised her hand.

"Yes?" Briar called on her.

"My name is Mimi Carlson, with the Rogers Park Resource Center. What population does Adult Protective Services work with?

"Although anyone can call the Hotline," Brian explained, "Adult Protective Services investigates abuse and neglect of elderly or dependent adults."

"Yes, I know," Carlson said. "But how is that population defined?"

"Elderly is considered to be anyone over sixty five years old. Although there is a lot of debate as to whether that particular cutoff is fair, that's the State regulation. Dependent adults are defined as individuals, between eighteen and sixty-five, who are dependent on other for their activities of daily living, or indirect activities of daily living."

"Reports of abuse or neglect for those people can be made on the Intake Hotline. Marlene Gregg devised the APS 24-hours Intake Hotline in 1992, as part of a move towards centralized intake for all Adult Services programs. My position is primarily Intake Social Worker on the Hotline. When I am not doing meetings such as this one, I am in the Bullpen providing information and referral, opening cases, and responding to office drop-ins. I also work with representative payee clients, individuals receiving public assistance, who need help managing money. I work from eight to five each week day, but we have on-call social workers available on evenings and weekends.

A balding gentleman, sitting across the table in a shirt and vest, raised his hand and said, "Jim Brainard, Drinking Driving Diversion Program."

"Yes, Jim, "Briar invited.

"How many calls do you get each month?"

"We estimate between 1200 and 1500 calls a month. Out of those calls, we probably open between twenty and thirty cases each month.

"Wow", Brainard said.

"Yes, indeed," said Briar.

"My two colleagues in the Bullpen are Patrick Brennan and Bob Foster, whose positions are Urgent Response Intake Social Workers. In addition to providing back up to my position, they will also go into the field to screen particularly vague or troublesome referrals, and respond to urgent situations. Both Brennan and Foster have psychiatric hold authority, meaning they can place on a psychiatric hold any individual deemed either to be a danger to themselves or others, or a gravely disabled adult. They will often consult with and do home visits with other social workers in the division, when there is a question of a psychiatric hold.

"There are also two APS Case Management Social Workers. If an Adult Protective Services case is opened, these workers provide case management for up to three months. They investigate allegations of abuse or neglect, and they work to try to help clients, their families and friends, obtain resources or make life adjustments to resolve whatever problem was presented to APS. If within the three months the problem is not solved, the case may be referred to one of the other units for further service. The Case Management Social Workers are Sollie Rivers and Emma Hayes.

"Actually, cases are often opened and closed on a repeated basis. Many of the individuals referred to APS have chronic physical or mental problems and dysfunctions they've taken a lifetime to develop. Many of these problems can not be resolved in three months, but are not appropriate for the other divisions. Those clients end up being recycled through the system – often time and time again.

"The APS unit also had one Conservatorship Investigator. Arielle Davis conducts investigations, and prepares the petitions filed in Superior Court, for cases involving individuals whom APS believes needs a conservator. A deputy public guardian, who can manage and protect the conservatee's welfare and assets, is assigned if Superior Court agrees with Adult Protective Services.

"Finally, the unit has one Public Health Nurse, who manages an abbreviated caseload which entrails more medical components that psychosocial ones. In addition to her own caseload, the nurse is expected to provide medical consultation for the other social workers. Our nurse is named Rhonda Pagan.

"I have a question," spoke up a dark-haired woman in a pants suit.

"Yes," Briar said.

"I'm Michelle Taylor, from the American Red Cross."

"Sure Michelle. What's your question?"

How long does it take for a social worker to go out on a case once it is referred to the hotline?"

"It depends on the situation and the urgency," Briar said. "We have the capability of getting out anytime between four hours and ten days. If it's an emergency situation, Bob Foster or Patrick Brennan can get out right away. If it is a serious situation, but there does not to be immediate danger, a case manager can get out with three days. If the situation is not serious, or if it appears to be chronic, we'll go out from five to ten days.

"We also have social workers who are on-call through the hotline for nights and weekend. These social workers are paid an overtime formula to be able to respond to situations on the phone on in person 24-hours a day. Marlene believes it's important that the public be able to reach a social worker at any time, without having to deal with an answering machine or service. On the hotline, we don't even have voice mail."

Jame Kimure then spoke up. "What if we don't want to make a referral, but we just want to consult about a potentially abusive situation: can we call simply to consult?"

"Of course, "Briar said. " You all are mandated reporters, meaning you are mandated by the state of California to report any incident of abuse or neglect become confused. You are all welcome to simply call and talk about the situation, and we will try to advice you the best we can."

"Well, thank you very much, Donna," Kimure said. "We appreciate you take the time."

"Sure," Briar said, passing out business cards around the table. "The Intake Hotline is open twenty-four hours a day, seven days a week."

Back in Cedarwood City, Patrick Brennan climbed back into his county car, and drove across town to the Cedarwood County Department of Health. The Department included Adult Services, as well as the county hospital, public health, mental health, and a smattering of other public services.

As Brennan strode down the hall toward the Big Room and his desk, he ran into his supervisor, the quiet and cerebral Chuck Corley, Corley, whose hairline had begun to recede slightly, wore his typical colored shirt and corresponding woolen tie. A soft spoken Buddhist with a seemingly indefatigable capacity for finding the good in people and situations, Corley had spent the last four years developing the quick-response capability, the efficiency, and the team-orientation which had come to characterize the APS unit.

"So, how'd it go with Mrs. Hirose?" asked Corley quietly.

"Okay. It took us a while, but we finally got her out of the house. Good thing, too, because the last thing she needs is Psychiatric Emergency."

"Good!" Corley said. "So, where did she go?"

"We found a cousin, who agreed to take her in for a while. The cousin lives in Corning. I figured I'd fill out a referral, and we'd have someone follow her for a while, and help the family figure out what to do with her."

"They posted the house?"

"Oh, yeah..! What a mess! Structural damage, no runnin' water, rodents; the whole works! It's funny..."Brennan paused. "This woman was well known in the community. She'd go to the senior center; she'd go shopping for herself. My guess is she spent most of the time away from her house, either none of her neighbors knew the condition of the house, or they just never said anything – until now."

"Yes, it's amazing," Corley said, in his usual understated manner. "Go ahead and write up the referral, and I'll give it to Emma."

"She'll be good for Mrs. Hirose." Brennan started to turn to go and then stopped and said. "By the way, Chuck, have you heard anything about the car?

"I put in the request last week," Corley sighed. "We'll just have to wait and see."

"Well, it seems pretty basic," Brennan complained. "The car needs washing, so I think I should just go get it washed, and get reimbursed through petty cash.

"I know," Corley sympathized, flashing his "go with the flow" smile. "It seems pretty simple, but I don't know what else I can do about it! Accounting just doesn't know if petty cash is set up to reimburse employees to wash the car. Reportedly, the motor pool is supposed to wash it."

"Yeah, well they obviously don't. I swear, that white car is beginning to look more like a gray car. It's actually sort of embarrassing t' be driving around in it. Somehow they can fly Morley (County Manager Ronald Morely) to a conference in Honolulu, but they can't find a way to reimburse me for a car wash."

"I don't know what to tell you, Patrick," Corley said. "I'll let you know when I find out."

"Well, I won't hold my breath, that's for sure."

With twelve years of experience with the county under his belt, Brennan had become rather used to situations as the one on Tower Street. More intuitive than necessarily clinically skilled, Brennan relied on an analytical and pragmatic mind to make his assessments. A former seminarian and a licensed psychotherapist with a writer's background, Brennan was one of the few social workers who could actually type and use a word processor comfortably. Documentation came more easily to Brennan that most, and he was considered by many the best documenter in the unit, perhaps the division. Whereas most workers jotted down only the basic facts of the case, Brennan liked to paint a verbal picture in the case notes. He believed anyone picking up the case later should be able to gather a clear picture of the situation from the case notes alone – something usually not possible.

He would document Mrs. Hirose's eviction in the case notes, but in order to actually open a case to refer to Emma Hayes, he would need a typewriter. Thus, his search commenced.

Brennan hunted about the Big Rooms' maze of baffles for several minutes until he finally found a spare typewriter. Unfortunately, this particular one possessed the unique idiosyncrasies of an "e" and an "o" which would constantly skip while typing at regular speed. This required him to go back to the beginning of each line, and retype every "e" and "o" in it.

Several days later, Rhonda Pagan hung up the phone at her cubicle desk, and headed out the Big Room toward the conference room for the Thursday unit meeting. She had intended to arrive early for the meeting, but was sidetracked by a phone caller who had dialed her extension by mistake. She shrugged off the disruption, walking briskly down the hallway for the meeting. When she turned the doorknob and pushed open the door, she immediately met a loud and boisterous, "Congratulations!"

A long silvery streamer spelling out "Happy Wedding" hung from the ceiling of the room. Green palm trees, seagulls, and brightly colored leas provided a Hawaiian motif to the room, reminiscent of Rhonda's homeland. White paper plates arranged on the conference table, awaited a variety of hot dishes, muffins, cakes, and beverages covered the wooden surface. Each of the well-wishers – staff of the APS unit – wore paper hats matching the table settings. As they celebrated, the words to the "Hawaiian Wedding Song" played behind them on a portable cassette player.

Pagan's smile beamed brightly as she stood in mild shock at the reception. One by one her colleagues hugged her and congratulated her personally. Pagan had been with the unit only seven months, but her effort and dedication had already become readily appreciated by her colleagues – who had quickly become her friends.

"Emma!" Pagan scolded. "I should have known you'd be behind this. I should have never told you about the engagement. Geez…he only proposed last week."

"Well, now you know," a porcine, tan woman with a beautiful face and long flowing brown hair chuckled. "There are no secrets in this unit – especially if it provided potential for a party! By the way, sorry for the crank phone call, but I had to keep you out of the room a few minutes longer."

"That was you?" Pagan said. "I thought the voice sounded vaguely familiar."

"So, when's the wedding?" Patrick Brennan quizzed, and he wrapped his arms around the nurse, kissing her on the cheek.

"Probably next summer," Pagan confided. "Donald and I haven't set an exact date yet."

"So what's he waiting for?" chided an olive-skinned man with a brown pony tail behind his head. As he embraced her, he laughed. "You better get this in writing!"

"Geez, Sollie," Pagan said, slapping his arm. "Be nice."

"Yeah, Sollie," Donna Briar said, hugging Pagan tightly.

"Come on, Rhonda," Briar said, motioning toward a chair at the head of the table. "Come sit down."

"My God," Pagan gasped. "Who brought all this food?"

We all brought something," Briar said, motioning toward a chair at the head of the table, "even the men." Rivers and Brennan looked sheepishly at each other. "But Arielle made most of the casseroles, of course."

"Of course," Pagan said, blushing and teary-eyed. "Mmmmm! Arielle, it looks so wonderful! Thank you all so much!"

"Congratulations!" said Chuck Corley behind Pagan, who turned to receive his hug.

Arielle Davis, a large, dark-haired woman in a dark blue dress with white polka dots, began slicing an egg frittata as the unit staff sat around the table, in pursuit of the celebration.

Chapter 2
FEBRUARY

At 9:15 am in the Bullpen in the southwest corner of Adult Service's Big Room, Donna Briar answered the APS Intake Hotline on the third ring.

"Good Morning. Cedarwood Adult Services," she said, "can I help you?"

"Is this Adult Protective Services?" a male voice on the other end asked.

"Yes, this is Adult Protective Services," Briar returned. "Can I help you?"

"My name is Ross Feller from Psychiatric Services at Pinecrest Hospital."

"Yes, Ross, this is Diane Briar. I'm a social worker. What can I do for you?

"I need to report an incident which occurred on Saturday night."

"Okay," Briar assured him, "you can tell me."

"At about 7:30 pm, the Maple Creek Police Department brought in a man named Jim Lacy. Ever heard of him?

"Let me check the computer," Briar said, as she flipped through several screens of information on the computer terminal. "There's no trace of a Jim Lacy."

"Anyway, he's 63 years old, and he's been living at the Roadside Inn at Maple Creek, but last Saturday, for some reason, he was unable to pay his bill. He apparently did not want to leave his motel room, and when the police got there, he could not give them a plan for where he would go next, or how he'd support himself. So they brought him here."

Feller continued. "He is alert and oriented, but he is severely visually impaired, and somewhat confused, and quite close mouthed. He'd overweight, and short of breath, but he refused to allow a doctor to examine him. Even if he allowed it, he has no medical insurance."

"No medical insurance…" Briar marveled, "What kind of income does he have?

"It isn't clear," Feller said. "He would give us no information about his money, other than he expects a check from some bank in a few days. He was very guarded about his money, and would give us no information."

"Okay…," Briar continued expectantly, "so what do you need from us?"

"The psychiatrist could find no reason to keep him on a hold…he was not a danger to himself or others…"

"Well, what about as a gravely disabled adult," Briar questioned. "It sounds like he had no plan for providing his own food clothing and shelter…"

"Well, the doctor felt there was not enough reason to admit him…"

"No medical insurance, right?" Brian mumbled.

Silence answered her on the other end.

"So, what happened to Mr. Lacy?"

"We put him up at the Wayside Inn in Cedarwood City for the weekend. We had a local church bring him some groceries. We'd like you guys to go out and talk to him. The doctor thinks you should do something about it."

"Really…" said Briar, "can you give me any other information about him?"

"Sorry, but I do have the phone number for a Marge Rigby at the Roadside Inn, where the police found Mr. Lacy. She's the manager there. She might be able to give you more information."

"Okay…" said Briar…"thanks a lot…"

As Briar hung up the phone, she mumbled to Bob Foster, seated in his cubicle diagonally from her. "I smell a dump…"

"What's that?" the bearded Foster murmured over his shoulder lost in his own work.

"Pinecrest Hospital," Briar sneered, "instead of admitting a 63-year-old who is confused, blind, and with no visible means of support, they stuck him at the Wayside Inn, and called us."

"That sounds like the Pinecrest to me." Foster said. "Let me guess: he's on Medicaid."

"No insurance, actually," Briar said, "but you were close."

With her head-set fastened about her head, Briar dialed a number for the Roadside Inn. Marge Rigby answered, in a gravelly voice which belied a lifelong dependence on tobacco. Briar began probing the manager's memory concerning the latest referral to APS.

Rigby said Lacy came to live at the Roadside Inn about eighteen months years prior, on an August Monday. Everyday Mr. Lacy would walk to his bank near the motel, and take some cash out of his account. He would return to the motel, pay fifty dollars for the next day's stay.

Rigby said Lacy seemed to be able to negotiate his way about the neighborhood, despite his visual limitations. Once he familiarized himself with the neighborhood, Lacy would regularly eat at nice restaurants downtown. He took taxi cabs just about everywhere he would go. Rigby said she thought he just plain ran out of money.

Rigby recalled Lacy once mentioning he was from Arizona, out near Tucson or some other such place. She also thought he mentioned living in Las Vegas for several months before moving to Cedarwood County. However, she could not say why he chose Maple Creek as his final destination.

Rigby said last Tuesday, Lacy did not come into the office to pay his bill. Rigby waited until Thursday, since he had been such a good customer for so long. Finally, on Thursday night she approached him for the rent. He said he had no more money, but he was expecting a payment from his bank. Finally, Rigby told Lacy he would have to leave if the rent was not there by Saturday afternoon. He refused to vacate the room, insisting more money would be coming to him at any time. He refused to provide her any other information. Finally, Rigby had no choice but to call the police, which is how he ended up at Pinecrest Hospital.

"So, what do you think the source of his income was?" Briar asked.

"I don't know," said Rigby. "It must have been a pretty large sum of money at one time, to enable him to live the way he did."

"Did he ever mention any relatives or friends?"

"He once said he had a brother living somewhere in the southwest, but I don't really know. He stayed pretty much to himself."

"I see."

"I was sorry to have to call the police," said Rigby. "He really seemed to be nice man, until he ran out of money."

"Well, you have a business to run," said Briar, sympathizing with Rigby. "You tried to help him, but you also had to do what you did. You couldn't let him stay there forever."

"What's going to happen to him now?" asked Rigby.

"Well, we'll probably send a social worker out to see him, to find out what we can and help him somehow."

"Well, I hope you can. He was such a polite man."

"We'll do what we can for him," Briar assured her.

A week later, in the Bullpen, Bob Foster had just completed a call on the Intake Hotline. Brennan, who overheard, swiveled in his chair.

"Who's that?" asked Brennan at his desk, looking over some notes he had taken on a recent referral.

Foster, a tall Irish-American from Brooklyn who sat across from Brennan's cubicle, shook his head and exclaimed, "Jesus Christ…"

"Jesus Christ called?"

"Nah, some 70-year-old lady from Dalton City…"

"What did she want?"

"She wants someone to fix her toilet."

"Well, didn't you volunteer to run right out there with your wrench? After all, we're supposed to be "everything to everyone" at Adult Services."

"No, actually, I told her you'd do it, and I gave her your home number. Is that okay?"

"Oh, sure, I'm on my way!" Brennan giggled. "So what's wrong with her toilet?"

"It don't work," he said. "She keeps throwing banana peels down it, and can't understand why it don't work."

"Doesn't she know about plumbers and phone books?"

"Yeah, but she says she can't afford a plumber, even though she earns $3000 per month income, and she owns her house free and clear. She thinks she's entitled to free help since she's a senior. She says she can't understand why all these foreigners and drug addicts get all this help, but taxpaying citizens can't?

"Which bloody foreigners and drug addicts is she referring to?

"Oh, you know: the same old crap!" Foster grimaced. "She doesn't know what the hell she's talking about…nitwit!"

"Another satisfied customer…"

"Yeah," Foster said, "she'll probably call the board of supervisors, and we'll have to run out there with our Drano anyway."

Foster and Brennan chuckled at the whole conversation, something they had a predilection toward doing anyway. As Foster would say, "If you can't laugh at your clients, what damned good are they?"

Just then, Rhonda Pagan quietly approached the men. She smiled her brightest smile, and greeted them, "Good morning, guys."

Foster and Brennan glanced at each other warily. Brennan muttered, "Oh-oh…"

"What do you want?" Foster said in monotone.

"What do you mean?" Pagan asked coyly.

"You never smile like that unless you want something," Foster continued. "So…"

"Well, as a matter of fact," Pagan smiled. "I am going to need help from one of you."

The two men exchanged quizzical glances. "I need to finish this referral," Brennan asserted quickly. "I guess you're up, Bob!"

"I guess so," Foster said, raising his six foot, five-inch frame slowly from his chair.

"C'mon," Pagan – a good foot shorter than Foster – motioned with her hand. "Let's talk over at my desk."

In his twenty- one years with Cedarwood County Department of Health, Robert Michael Foster figured he had pretty much seen it all. Tall, rugged, a mixture of thinning red and gray hair atop his head and across his chin, Foster filled the role of sage father figure for the Big Room staff. Staff – including supervisors and administrators – regularly came to the Bullpen to seek his guidance and counsel on a number of matters. In addition to his past experience in mental health and the public guardian's office, Foster served a shop steward for the social worker's union. A former sergeant in the US Army in Germany, he possessed a keen radar for archaic rules and regulations, and ways to fit them in or around the real life situations APS often faced.

Pagan quickly told Foster the story of Leona Pendleton. Although nearly twenty-five years his junior, Pagan never felt intimidated about sharing her opinions with him – or anyone else in the unit. "I normally would give this woman time to see if she can respond to her needs," Pagan explained, "but I am afraid her medical condition is quickly approaching critical. She doesn't understand her condition, and she is not making the decisions she needs to in order to stay healthy."

"Sounds good to me," Foster said. "Why don't you let me look over the case notes, and we'll set up a time to go see her."

Two days later in a steady rain, Pagan and Foster cruised toward Shady Grove in the county Ford Tempo to determine whether Pendleton's medical needs had become enough to require hospitalization against her will.

"So, how are the wedding plans coming?" Foster asked, as they headed toward central Baldwyn.

"Oh, fine," Pagan responded.

"So, when is the wedding taking place?"

Pagan paused for a moment. "Uh…actually, we haven't set a precise date yet. We haven't been able to settle on the date or place yet. His family is from the north, so there is some disagreement about how all of this will commence."

"I see," Foster said, letting his left eyebrow raise inquisitively.

"Weddings…" Pagan sighed.

"Yeah, after my marriage, I've definitely concluded a wedding should be a once-in-a-lifetime event."

"Well, I'll be glad when it's over…" Pagan sighed wearily.

Foster's eyebrow cocked once more as Pagan stared absently out her window. He shook his head slightly, so she would not even notice.

"Anyway," Pagan said, changing the subject quickly. "I spoke with the nephew yesterday. His name is Marty, and he lives in Dover, about five hours to the east. He was given power of attorney about two years ago, so he pays her bills and sends her money on a regular basis. Apparently, she used to lose her bills in that apartment of hers. But he hasn't seen her in many months. He said he gave up long ago trying to change her ways; all he can manage now is to pay her bills.

"Swell," Foster said, "Well, at least we know the bills are paid. We'll just have to see what we'll do next. But what happens if she don't wanna let us in again?"

"Betty Major was going to arrange for a key, just in case."

"I'm not thrilled with entering someone's apartment against their will. Mrs. Penderblast...Pendergrass" Foster stumbled over the name.

"Pendleton.," Pagan corrected him.

"Pendleton…whatever…" Foster shrugged. "She's that bad off?"

"Majors thinks so," Pagan said. "She said some of the staff have complained about the smell, and Pendleton hardly every leaves her bed anymore."

"Oh, well…" Foster shrugged, "I guess we'll know when we get there."

When the pair from APS arrived, they were immediately greeted by one of the cleaning staff for the apartment building. On instruction from Betty Major, a middle-aged woman named Lupe led Foster and Pagan up to the third story apartment. When the staff woman knocked on the apartment, a gravelly voice immediately shouted from inside.

"Go away! Leave me alone!"

"At least she's home," Pagan quipped.

Lupe stepped away from the door. "She's been like this for days," the staff woman announced. "She just keeps getting worse and worse, and the apartment's a mess. Somebody has to do something."

"We'll see what we can do to help her," Foster assured her.

Lupe slipped a brass key into the doorknob, and opened the door. She led Pagan and Foster into the room. "These people are here to help you," said Lupe. "They want to talk with you."

Well, I don't want to talk to them," the raspy voice called.

Pagan and Foster stepped further inside the apartment, as Lupe handed Foster the key. Pagan carried a medical kit, which included a blood pressure monitor and a stethoscope. Foster carried his leather folder, containing the psychiatric hold documents, and a cell phone. Toward the left of the room they found an elderly woman, lying in her bed next to a large picture window overlooking the park. Her gray hair hung limply on her shoulders, and her face wore an expression of rage, confusion, and embarrassment; as she raised her hands to admonish the APS workers, her arms trembled. It appeared she may have laid in her bed for quite some time, perhaps days. The room smelled of dust, must, and urine; her sheets looked damp and worn. Food trays covered with wrappers and dishes lay on the floor next to the bed. Throughout the room clothes and books and newspapers and food wrappers lay scattered. Through the open bathroom door – as Betty Major had described – the APS workers could see bags and boxes stacked inside the tub, evidence that Pendleton had not bathed in a very long time.

"Good morning, Mrs. Pendleton," Rhonda Pagan introduced. "My name is Rhonda. I'm a nurse. I talked to you through the door the other day, don't you remember?"

"No, I don't" the old woman grumbled.

"This is Bob," Pagan continued. "He's a social worker. We're here to see what we can do for you."

"Go away. I don't want you here," the woman wheezed. "I don't need any help."

"Are you having trouble breathing, Mrs. Pendleton?" Pagan asked.

"No, I'm not!" Pendleton answered, coughing traumatically. "I'm just mad because you came into my room. Now, get out!"

"But you look sick, Mrs. Pendleton," said Pagan. "Could I examine you, to make sure you're okay?"

"No! Go away!" said Pendleton. "I'm going to see my doctor next week."

"You haven't seen your doctor in a long time, Mrs. Pendleton," Pagan interjected. Foster marveled at the young nurse's patient. "I spoke to him few days ago. That's why I'm here. Your doctor wanted to make sure you're okay."

Mrs. Pendleton eyed the young nurse, as if trying to see beyond the imagined charade. But before she could say anything further, Foster asked the woman, "So, what happened to your room?"

Pendleton hesitated for a moment, and then answered, "I've been sick. My nephew is coming to help me clean it next week."

"When was the last time you saw your nephew, Mrs. Pendleton?"

Pendleton paused, as if trying to gather the memory.

Pagan answered the question herself. "It's been a long time. I spoke to him yesterday."

"Well, what business do you have calling my nephew? Who the hell are you, anyway?"

"She told you, ma'am," Foster responded. "I am a social worker, and she's a nurse. We're here from the county health department, and we're here to see how you're doing. We were told you were sick, and you might need some medical attention."

"Who told you? Who told you to call here?" Pendleton shrieked, wildly.

"It doesn't matter, ma'am," Foster answered. "Now, if you just let the nurse examine you, we can leave you alone!"

"I'm not letting any nurse examine me!" Pendleton shouted. "Now, go away!"

"Ma'am, we can't go until we find out how you are."

"I'm fine!" she yelled. "Now, go away!"

"Will you answer some questions?" Foster asked.

"No! Go away!"

"Do you know what day today is?" Foster continued.

"Of course I do."

"What is today's date?" Foster asked.

"I don't have to answer that!" Pendleton griped.

"What's your birthday?" Foster pushed on.

"I don't have to tell you!"

"Tell me your address!"

"I don't have to tell you anything! You leave me alone!! Get the hell out of here!!!"

All through Foster's questions, Pagan watched the old woman. Finally, she pulled Foster aside, and they both stepped outside the apartment.

The public health nurse said, "Do you notice her shortness of breath?

"Yeah," answered Foster, "she don't sound good."

"It sounds like her lungs are congested. She's perspiring, which means she may have a fever. Also, her legs are swollen with edema; she may be having circulation problems, or even trouble with her kidneys."

"How can you be sure, though? She won't let you examine her."

"Let's try again. If she'll at least let me touch her, take her pulse, I can get a better idea."

Rhonda Pagan returned to Mrs. Pendleton, with Foster following behind. "Mrs. Pendleton, if you would just let me take your pulse and your blood pressure."

Pendleton coughed. "Who are you?" she asked, somewhat quietly. She seemed to be losing some of her energy.

"I'm the nurse from the county. I've come to check on your health."

The old woman seemed dazed, and she looked toward the floor, as if trying to recall some information. Pagan slowly approached the woman, and reached out to grasp her wrist. As the nurse held her wrist, she leaned closer toward the old woman, trying to get a look under the scarf across her forehead. At first Pendleton instinctively allowed Pagan to hold her arm. But in a moment she seemed to remember what was going on, and she wrenched her wrist away. "I told you to go away!" she screamed. "You go away or I'll call the police."

"She's very warm," Pagan addressed Foster, "and I can hear the congestion in her lungs. That wound on her forehead doesn't look very good, either."

"What happened to your forehead, Mrs. Pendleton?" Foster asked.

"Nothing..!" Pendleton roared. "My head is cold!"

Pagan eased over to the social worker. "She needs to get to the hospital," she said. "She might have pneumonia."

"Ma'am," continued Foster, "the nurse thinks you're very sick, and you need medical help."

"I'll see my doctor next week."

"We already talked about that, Mrs. Pendleton," Pagan said. "You've made no attempt to see your doctor. But if you like, we could take you to a doctor, to have you examined."

"I don't need a doctor!" she screamed. "Now, get out of my house, before I call the police."

This time Foster led the way out to the hall. Pagan looked at him in the eye. "I can't leave her here like this," she said.

"Okay," Foster said. "She's clearly confused, and very paranoid and agitated. She's in medical distress, and her behavior and condition of the room would confirm her dementia. She ain't capable of managing her money, and she ain't capable of arranging her own medical care. That's good enough for me."

Foster took his cell phone, dialing the number for Psychiatric Emergency for the county hospital.

"Hello, Jan?" Foster said.

"This is Jan Cowles," answered a young woman, the triage nurse for Psychiatric Emergency.

"This is Bob Foster, Adult Protective Services."

"Hi, Bob, what's going on?"

"Guess what?" said Foster.

"Let me guess…" the woman said, "you've got someone for us."

"Yeah, this is an eighty-six year old woman who appears to be in medical distress. She has congestion in her lungs, she seems to have a fever, and she seems to have a nasty open wound over her left eye, but she won't let the nurse examine her. She appears very agitated, confused, and paranoid; she hasn't seen her own doctor in about four years. The nurse feels she needs to get to a hospital, and I don't think she has the wherewithal to manage it herself."

"What's her name?"

"Leona Pendleton. She lives ay 285 Norfolk Street in Baldwyn, Apartment 314."

"What kind of medical insurance does she have?"

"I don't know," Foster muttered. He looked at Pagan. "Insurance…?"

"Medicare," she answered.

"Medicare," Foster repeated.

"Hold on," said Cowles, "let me give you an ETA."

Foster paused for a moment, rolling his eyes toward Pagan, and then Cowles announces, "The ambulance will be there in about twenty minutes. She should probably go to the Medical ER first, right?"

"Definitely," Foster said. "Thanks for your help, Jan."

"Any time," Cowles answered.

Foster gave Pagan the ETA. "Should we tell her where she is going?"

Pagan asked

"Let's wait until the ambulance gets here. The less time she has to think about it, the less time she has to work up a froth."

Pagan nodded. Foster found a table and chair in the third floor lobby, and took the moment to fill out the "Application for 72-hour hold," form. The form required Foster to document how the client in question came to his attention, and the factors that support his decision to have her hospitalized against her will. The form requires Foster to use clinical terms, so the receiving psychiatrist understand Foster knows of what he writes. Foster did not have to positively diagnose Mrs. Pendleton, but merely presented enough reasons to demonstrate if he did not place her on a hold, she would be in grave danger.

Just as Foster signed his name to the form – which, of course, did not leave enough space for any legible writing – the elevator door opened, revealing a wheeled gurney, followed by two paramedics – one male, one female – from Hillstar Ambulance Company. Foster led them into the room, where they found Mrs. Pendleton. One tall, young, blonde male paramedic, perusing the situation, looked haughtily at Foster and Pagan. "What's her name?" he said. Out loud in from of her.

"This is Mrs. Pendleton," Pagan said. "She…"

"I'll handle this," the man said. The name tag on his coveralls read, "Boll"

"Hello, Mrs. Pendleton. I'm from the ambulance company. Do you need to go to the hospital?"

"No!" Pendleton of course shouted. "Now, all of you get out of my apartment."

Boll looked at Pagan incredulously and demanded, "On what basis are we transporting this woman?"

"I'm Rhonda Pagan, a public health nurse from Adult Protective Services. This is Bob Foster, a social worker. We're here because this woman is ill, she is confused, she is paranoid, and she needs medical attention, but she won't go. She has congestion in her chest, a fever, and an open wound over he left eye."

"Did you examine the wound?" Boll quizzed.

"She wouldn't let me…"

"But if she doesn't want to go," Boll said, looking down his nose, "we have no authority to take her. We can't be moving her furniture and all her stuff…"

Meanwhile, Bob Foster's brow furrowed, as it did when his tolerance for petulant professional conduct reached its threshold. He stepped forward toward the paramedic, raising himself to his full 6'5" height. The other paramedics – not as tall as Boll – eyed Foster warily.

"Look, Mr. Balls…" Foster purposely misspoke.

"That's Boll. Howard Boll." The young paramedic murmured.

"Look, Mr. Boll, I'm authorized by the county to place Mrs. Pendleton on a psychiatric hold – under the Welfare and Institutions Code – if I assess her to be gravely disabled, or a danger to herself, or both. She's not responding rationally, and she very well may have a serious medical emergency with which she cannot deal. This is my responsibility, and I am willing to take it." Foster presented the form.

Boll took the form, and glanced at it momentarily. "I guess so…" he shrugged, showing it to the female.

"I guess so," she responded.

"Swell!" Foster steamed.

The other paramedic cleared a path among the furniture and the garbage and the papers and the books. They wheeled the gurney to the bed, and although Pendleton screamed, "No! No!" and "I'll call the police!" the whole time, she lacked the strength to put up a good fight.

As they lifted Pendleton onto the gurney, the female paramedic - nearest Pendleton's head - removed the scarf, and gasped," Phew! Oh, boy, that's bad. This smells like it might be infected. How did you guys know?

"We're supposed to know," Pagan shot, astounding everyone with her sudden force. "That's our jobs…now let's go!"

The tall medic said nothing more, as he seemed to finally realize Pagan and Foster knew exactly what they were doing.

Several days later, Emeline Marie Hayes arose from her cubicle and slowly wandered over the few steps to the Bullpen. A case manager for APS, Hayes played the role of the Bohemian soul for the unit. A lovely face surrounded by cascading brown hair over a corpulent frame, Hayes normally wore flowing, earth-tone clothing and Birkenstock sandals. Always a brilliant diagnostician, Hayes had also become a fierce advocate for individual rights. She believed deeply in the responsibility of government to provide for the basic needs of disadvantaged people, but she also fervently defended the individual's right to decide his or her own destiny.

Hayes had initially been given authority to place people on psychiatric holds, but she soon turned it down, as she did not believe there were any circumstances in which she – in good conscience – could bring someone to the hospital involuntarily.

In addition to her work at APS, Hayes and her husband regularly volunteered at the local soup kitchens on weekends. She stayed consistently informed about legislation pending on the state and local level, which might affect the lives of low-income people with whom she regularly worked.

"How's it going, Emma?" Brennan asked, as he glanced up from his computer terminal.

"Okay," Hayes returned.

"How's the boat?"

"Ray and I got up to the lake this weekend," she to him with her sweet smile. "It was beautiful."

"It's a houseboat, right?"

"Yeah", she said. "We keep it up there for vacations."

"Weren't you thinking of moving into the boat permanently?" Brennan probed.

"Yeah, but that means I would have to find a job up near the lake. It's pretty rural, not many opportunities for social workers."

"Too bad," Brennan consoled. "Sounds like it would be great?"

"Maybe some day," Hayes mused. "Anyway, remember Mrs. Hirose?"

"Who?" Brennan asked absent-minded

"You know, the woman in the horrible house."

"Oh, yeah…Skip's aunt. How are things going?"

"It looks like Mrs. Hirose had some money in her bank account," Hayes revealed. "They're going to use it to clean up the house. She might be able to return to the house in a month or so."

"Is she going to be able to live there by herself?"

"Actually, they're talking about having Skip move in with her."

"Oh, yeah..?" Brennan questioned skeptically. "Skip doesn't seem exactly like the salt of the earth to me."

"Yeah…I know," Hayes said. "But I think it's worth a try. Otherwise, she'd probably have to go to a board and care."

"What does Skip do for a living, anyway," Brennan quizzed.

"I'm not sure..." Hayes grinned. "He seems to be between po-sitions...perpetually."

"Yeah, I'm sure..."

At that moment, Chuck Corley ambled into the Bullpen. "I put a case on your desk, Emma," he said, "about Mr. Lacy, at the Way-side Inn. Donna has arranged for him to stay there for a few more days, and the on-call worker brought him some food. But I'd like you to get there in the next couple of days."

"What's the situation?" Hayes asked.

Briar piped up from behind her cubicle baffle. "I took the refer-ral, Em. I can tell you about it."

"I'll talk to you later, Patrick," Hayes said, she pulled a chair next to Briar.

The following Wednesday morning Ari Davis, knocked gently but firmly on the door of Chuck Corley's office. "Come on in, Ari," Corley motioned.

"Hi, Chuck," David said. "I wanted to know a little bit about Milton Bates. He's in the hospital?"

"Yes," Corley said, "we got the conservatorship referral from Pinecrest Hospital. Apparently Mr. Bates' wife's body had been found in her bedroom, where she apparently suffered an embolism and died some time previously. They discovered the wife only be-cause neighbors found Mr. Bates wandering around, very disori-ented in his Brystol neighborhood yesterday. The police discovered the body, and took Bates to the hospital on a hold. The psychiatrist believes he has moderate to severe dementia. Neighbors told police Bates' wife used to manage the household, and now he apparently doesn't know what to do with himself."

"Does Bates have a set of keys?" Davis asked

"I don't know..."

"Well, I'll wander out to the hospital, and see what I can find out. Maybe the neighbors will know something."

Ari Davis made her way back to her cubicle, just beyond the Bullpen. A multi-patterned and multi-colored handmade quilt on a cotton field of navy blue draped over her south partition. A stuffed giraffe and a tericloth elephant – stitched by Davis' own hand – sat a top her bookshelf. Davis always provided some amazing creations of stitching for the adult fund raffle or the Christmas boutique. Routinely, as a Rhonda Pagan's party, Davis would provide some elaborate quiche or decadent cake for the unit's delight. She saw herself as the mother of the unit, bringing many of the motherly qualities – welcomed or otherwise – to her cases, her colleagues, and her clients.

While Davis prepared for her home visit, a white Chevy van maneuvered down the highway toward the city of Shelton. The van displayed a county emblem on the door, under which block letters spelled out the word, "Animal Control". Sollie Rivers, APS case manager, accompanied Mel Morales, Animal Control officer, to the scene of another potential case.

Rivers rode in Morales' van because of another little snafu exercised by county administration. Few of the county's bumbles could surprise Rivers anymore, no matter how numerous or varied. Nevertheless, he always managed to find – or at least, create – some entertainment out of them.

In this case, the Health Department arranged a major purchase for the Department's motor pool. All the cranky, creaky Chevettes and T-1000's – many of which seemed to be held together with chewing gum and good wishes – had been replaced by a bright new fleet of Tauruses and Oldsmobiles. Unfortunately, administration forgot to have the vehicles registered either with the county motel pool or the Department of Motor Vehicles. Until properly registered, the cars could not be used.

So, when Morales – a squat little man with a handlebar mustache – called the APS hotline to have a social worker accompany him on a home visit, Bob Foster had to ask Morales if the social worker could "get a ride" with him. "We're outa cars," Foster explained, far too jaded to worry about the potential embarrassment of the situation.

So, on the day of the visit, Morales stopped by the front of the Health Department, honked his horn, and Rivers came out for the ride.

Soloman David Rivers served as the lightning rod for politically sensitive cases for APS. When expected, these kinds of cases normally came to him; when not expected, they often seemed to find him anyway. Rivers exuded the right combination of courage and con to handle these assignments. With dark, boyish good looks and a rapid, animated sense of humor, Rivers often flew by the seat of his pants. Somehow, even in the most pressure-filled situation, Rivers would land on his feet, somehow able to steer the course of his case to an appropriate conclusion.

"So, are you Mexican?" Morales bluntly asked him, observing his dark skin and long hair, pulled tightly behind his head in a short pony tail.

"No," Rivers answered, apparently unaffected by Morales' blunt question. "My mother was Jewish, and my father had Pomo Indian blood."

"Indian, huh…?" Morales said.

"Yep," Rivers answered, pulling his leather jacket around his collar. "Why?"

"Just wondering, that's all," Morales shrugged.

"So, do you like doing animal control?" Rivers asked.

"Yeah, it's okay," Morales told him. "You can get into some pretty hairy situations…get it?" Morales laughed at his pun

"Yeah, yeah," Rivers grinned half-heartedly.

"One winter morning," Morales recalled fondly, "we found some creature hidden in a clothes dryer, in a house up in the Brystol hills. The creature had apparently crawled in for some warmth, and when the owner turned it on, she freaked and called animal control. We never did figure out exactly what it was; when we opened the dryer, the thing bolted, and ran out into the woods. It looked like some kind of weasel or something."

Morales' anecdotes continued until the van crossed the Shelton City limits. The case they pursued had already been labeled, "The Cat Woman of Shelton." For years the Cat Woman – a 77-year-old woman named Eloise Campbell – had been a nuisance to the Shelton office of Code Enforcement, and its chief Carol Horsely. Horsely had been attempting to corral the Cat Woman for years. Now apparently, she finally had her chance

Dubbed the Cat Woman because of the legions of feral feline attracted to her Shelton hills home, Eloise Campbell had became a rather infamous gadfly to the community. The former city council member was known for her eccentric manner and her even more eccentric ideas. For example, she once tried to initiate the use of mounted patrols for the police department, thinking it would add a stately air to the city. The fact that none of the police force could ride, and city maintenance had no experience cleaning up the equine excrement did little to dissuade her idea. Horsely, a long time employee of the city, had numerous run-ins with Campbell over the years; revenge, apparently, ranked high among Horsely's motivations in her quest for the Cat Woman. Horsely had tried numerous attempts to have Campbell's house posted as uninhabitable, and to have Campbell conserved. But so far, she had been unable to find a doctor to side with her.

This latest chapter concerned a complaint by the Cat Woman's neighbor regarding Campbell's home on Edinburgh Street. The complaint cited as many as twenty-two cats roaming about the house. The stench reached the street, the neighbor complained, and cat feces littered both the house and the yard. The noisy howling kept the neighbor up many nights; he called Campbell a nuisance, and called her home a health hazard.

Consequently, Mel Morales came equipped with several cat cages, which he would use to trap and remove as many ferals as possible to the animal shelter. Morales and Rivers planned to meet Horsely, her colleagues from code enforcement, and staff from county environmental health, the fire department, and the police department. At 10:30 am, in one fell swoop, the officials hoped to trap the cars, examine the house, and evaluate the competency of Eloise Campbell.

"Sounds like a pretty drastic operation for a bunch of cats," Rivers said.

"Don't kid yourself," Morales said gravely. "We could be facing a real health hazard here. This isn't the first time we've tangled with the Cat Woman."

Rivers shrugged, "Whatever…"

Apparently, no one had placed a priority on confidentiality for the case. When Morales and Rivers rolled up, they found a TV Channel 7 News van parked outside the Campbell home. Apparently someone had "leaked" word to the TV station of the imminent sting taking place at the Cat Woman's house. "Slow news day?" Rivers mumbled to Morales.

Two police cars, a city code enforcement vehicle, and two other county sedans from the environmental health department; in all nine city and county officials – along with the reporter and camera man from Channel 7 – gathered outside the Cat Woman's lair. In fact, only one crucial entity was missing.

"She's not home," said Carol Horsely, a stern woman with a Code Enforcement badge on the lapel of her gray rain coat. "I knocked on the door and no one answered. There are several cats on the property, however, and the side garage door is open. But the front door is closed and locked."

"Well," added one of the uniformed officers. "We can't enter the house if she's not home."

"But", said Morales, "we can at least begin setting the traps."

"Damn! I thought we'd get her today," Horsely complained.

One of the corner of his eye, Sollie Rivers noticed the TV reports approaching the official gathering. Normally happy to garner such attention, Rivers immediately decided discretion would be the safer course. "I'll go see if I can get some information from a neighbor," Rivers volunteers.

"Good idea, Sollie," Horsely chimed. Rivers left the huddle at the reporter managed to snare Morales for an on-camera interview.

Rivers – dressed in his customary shirt and tie, which usually accompanied a leather jacket or a woolen sweater – jogged across the street in a diagonal direction. He headed toward a house whose car was parked in the driveway. The neighbor – a Mrs. Meredith, herself in her sixties – invited the social worker inside, and willingly divulged all she knew about the notorious neighbor.

Meredith said she had been a neighbor of Campbell's for many years. Although she admitted to seeing cats around her yard now and again, she did not perceive the situation to be as bade as reports indicated. Clearly, Mrs. Meredith was not the neighbor who snitched.

"It was probably her next door neighbor," she said, pointing to the green house with the impeccably manicured lawn. "Mr. Gardena and Mrs. Campbell have been feuding for years."

"Do you know where Mrs. Campbell might be now?" Rivers asked.

"I don't know," Meredith responded. "I saw her standing at the bus stop down the street earlier today."

"So she can take the bus?" Rivers confirmed.

"Oh, yes, she seems quite healthy. And although Mr. Gardena complains about her, she has always been very nice to me."

"Does she have any family anywhere?"

"She has a daughter who lives north of here. I believe her name is Doris."

"Do you happen to know her phone number?"

"No, I'm afraid. But she comes to visit about once a week."

Handing her one of his business cards, Rivers said, "If you see her and if you think of it, would you give her this? I'd like to talk to her if I can."

"Certainly," Mrs. Meredith assured him.

Rivers thanked Meredith and returned to the huddle near Campbell's house. Morales had apparently finished with the TV reporter, and had returned from the back of the house.

Rivers told Horsely what the neighbor had said, and told her he would return to the house another time, to try to talk with Eloise Campbell. "I don't know," Rivers said, "but from what the neighbor said, she doesn't sound like she would be conservable. She sounds like she is perfectly able to fend for herself. She apparently took the bus out of here earlier this morning. I think the only way you might gain some leverage over her is if the house is postable."

"Well, it probably isn't," Horsely said, clearly frustrated. "It definitely smells, and there are cat feces in the garage. But from what we can see of the house from the window, it appears fairly Spartan – definitely not the trash heap we've seen elsewhere. So when do you think you'll get back here, Sollie?"

"I don't know," he responded, "probably next week some time, preferably without the circus."

"Maybe I should come with you..." Horsely began.

"Thanks, Carol," Rivers said, holding up his hand, "but I think maybe I should go by myself. I think I'll be able to get more information and cooperation alone."

"Oh, really..." Horsely said, frowning a bit. "Very well, Sollie...if you think so..."

"Yeah, I do," Rivers insisted.

"But if you see anything in the house you think we should know about, you'll let us know, won't you?"

"Of course, Carol," Rivers responded, shaking the Code Enforcement officer's hand.

Rivers motioned to Morales. "Are you done?"

"Yeah, I laid out some traps in her back yard. We should be able to collect them later."

The two climbed back into the county van. As Morales started the ignition, he rubbed his chin and pondered aloud. "Maybe I shouldn't have allowed myself on TV."

"What's that?" Rivers asked.

"The TV camera...maybe I shouldn't have let them talk to me."

"Why not...?" Rivers snickered. "Don't you like being on TV?"

"Yeah, except I've been working undercover for the last few weeks, trying to break up a cockfighting ring. I'm getting pretty close, too. I hope nobody sees me on TV."

Rivers look out the window, and tried to hold his laugh. He rolled his eyes, and half-heartedly reassured Morales. "I'm sure it'll be fine…" Rivers snickered.

Two days later, after knocking on the front door several times, Arielle Sarah Davis walked swiftly down the front brick steps. She stepped through a high wooden gate which led along the side of the Bates house to the back yard. For a woman of her size, she could move with remarkable speed and determination. She had already been by the hospital to see Mr. Bates, who remained in a very disoriented and delusional state. Hospital staff reported they had found no keys on him, nor had the police mentioned finding any.

Rather than visit the neighbors immediately, Davis decided to check the house entrances to see if any were open. Ari Davis always seemed to be able to find her way into the house of a proposed conservatee – whether she had keys or not. Davis attributed this point to the dementia that most of her clients had. She would say they would almost always forget to close or lock doors, making it rather simple to enter the homes.

Actually, Davis' tactics had come under question more than once from police and colleagues, concerned about violations of personal rights. Davis' bull-dog persistence in her pursuit of information and safety verged on the controversial. But Davis would always justify what others might regard an invasion of privacy, or illegal entry. For the most part, because she had been so effective for so long at gathering information for conservatorship petitions, supervisors and managers would normally overlook her questionable methods.

In contrast to the Bates' front yard, which appeared neat, fairly opulent, and well groomed, the back yard looked stark, under grown, and dry: as if no one had attended to its maintenance for a substantial period of time. The back façade featured a sliding glass patio door, a wooden screen over a narrow back door leading to the kitchen. Cobwebs outlined both doors, indicating neither had been used with any regularity or currency.

Carrying a sizeable leather briefcase on her arm, Davis checked the glass door, and then the kitchen door. She pulled the screen open and, turning the tarnished door knob, pushed the kitchen door open. "Tsk...tsk...tsk," she murmured. She walked into the kitchen, and through the living room. While neat and orderly, the house maintained a dark and dank atmosphere, enhanced by an eery silence. The stench of death – an essence with which Davis had become quite familiar – hovered slightly but absolutely, and intensified as Davis moved toward the back bedrooms. She found Mrs. Bates bedroom apparently as it had been left: letters and documents cascading from the rumpled bed onto the floor, where the older woman had fallen. Streaks of blood stained the carpet where the body had laid.

Davis shook her head again. "Tsk...tsk...tsk..." she muttered audibly, then went to work. Like a bat using radar to find its night-flying prey, Davis seemed to focus precisely in on the locations of pertinent information on her client. She gathered an assortment of documents from the dresser and stuffed them into her briefcase. At the bottom of a closet in what appeared to be a home office, she found an unlocked strong box containing a will and other legal documents. She emptied those contents into the briefcase as well.

On the bookshelf in the same room, she discovered two scrap books filled with photographs and clippings concerning the couple. Apparently Mrs. Bates had run for city council several times and actually served in her younger days – becoming one of the first women to serve on a city council in Cedarwood County. Mr. Bates, on the other hand, had been a chemist for a local medical equipment manufacturer, and had won several scientific awards for his developments.

On the oak desk in the home office teetered what appeared to be a stack of letters from friends and acquaintances. It looked as if Mrs. Bates had intended to answer them at some point, but apparently never had the chance. Davis hoped contact with these people would reveal additional information she would need for the petition.

On a set of pegs on the wall in the kitchen, she found a spare house key, the keys to the strong box, and the keys to a Buick Sierra, parked downstairs in the garage. From it, Davis confiscated the car registration and license.

As Ari Davis ambled her way back up the stairs into the kitchen, she suddenly shrieked as a deep male voice shouted at her, "Stop where you are! Identify yourself!"

Davis turned slowly to face a uniformed Brystol police officer holding his nightstick at arms length in front of him. He appeared young, with short brown hair, and a pencil thin mustache.

"I am Officer Quinton of the Brystol police. Identify yourself!"

"Oh…Officer," Davis sighed, holding her chest, "you scared the bejeebers out of me!"

"Ma'am, I'll ask you once more: please identify yourself…"

"I'm sorry, officer," she said, sweetly. She pointed to the county badge clipped of her blue sweater, and said, "I am Ari Davis, investigator for the Public Guardian's office. I am here about the Bates' case. Were you involved in the incident yesterday?"

"Yes," he answered, "but the neighbors just called, saying they saw some strange woman entering through the Bates' gate. Do you normally enter your client's homes through the back door?"

"Only when I don't have a key," Davis said, unfazed by the officer's distress. "The hospital said there was no key when Bates was admitted. Fortunately, I found a back door open. I am gathering information for the conservatorship petition I will be writing on Mr. Bates.

Quinton looked at the briefcase she held out, glanced again at the badge. "Very well," the officer said, "but next time, why don't you call us ahead of time to let us know what you're doing."

"Oh, sure, officer," Davis said, quickly turning the subject of the conversation. "So, you're the one who found Mrs. Bates?"

"Yes, "Quinton said. "You saw the room…?"

"Yes…quite a mess, huh?"

"Very much; she apparently burst a blood vessel in her head, and then hit her forehead against the corner of the bed when she fell. The man was so out of it, he didn't know what to do; apparently he let the body lie there for at least a day or two. If the neighbors hadn't have spotted him wandering up and down the street, the body might still be there."

"Well, I've been to the hospital to see Mr. Bates," she said.

"How's he doing?"

"He's still pretty confused. I'm going to complete the petition for temporary conservatorship as quickly as possible, so we can place him in a safe environment right away. He doesn't have any other family?'

"Not as far as anyone knows," Quinton said. "The neighbors said the Bates never had children, so there is no next of kin. Both of them worked; she was on the city council for a number of years, while he worked as a chemist. They have a pretty good estate here."

"It looks like it. Well, Officer, we'll take good care of him."

"Well, don't let me keep you," he said, showing her to the front door.

"Thank you, Officer Quinton," David smiled, "thank you for your help."

Chapter 3
MARCH

Late on a sunny but cool March Friday morning, Emma Hayes knocked on the door of room sixteen at the Wayside Inn. This motel stood on the east side of Cedarwood City in a neighborhood featuring a host of seedy motels, low-rent housing projects, and decaying city parks. Only three motels –including the Wayside Inn – in the entire county would agree to accept county vouchers as payment, and allow county clients to occupy a room. Motel managers did not generally worry about the demeanor and behavior of the clients, as much as the number of weeks (or sometimes months) it could take the county accounting office to pay the motel bill. But the Wayside Inn management proved desperate enough to accept the county way of doing business. Although certainly not Shangri La, most clients preferred the Wayside Inn to the street.

Cottages comprising a series of off-pink duplexes – stretched around a U-shaped parking lot – formed the Wayside Inn. The motel office stood at the left end of the "U". Hayes stopped in at the office, where the manager – a Mr. Patel – indicated James Lacy occupied room sixteen. As she knocked, Hayes heard a muffled response from the other side of the door, a deep southwest twang which called "C'mon in."

Hayes turned the knob and stepped inside. Moldy walls surrounded a bed and dresser on a dank, dirty carpet. A TV perched on its stand next to the dresser, and a polyester arm chair rested next to the bed. In the arm chair lounged a rotund, red-faced older man, whom Hayes estimated weighed 275 pounds. A brown crew cut topped the long-jowl ruddy face. He wore a white cotton shirt with brown slacks, and a tan cowboy hat lay upon the far side of the bed cover. The man turned his head slowly toward the door as Hayes entered the room; his eyes squinted painfully as the shimmer of the Friday morning sun filled the otherwise shadowy cell.

"Mr. Lacy?" Hayes called gently, befitting her manner.

"Yes, Ma'am," Lacy answered.

"My name is Emma Hayes. I'm a social worker from the County of Cedarwood. I'm here to see how you're doing, and see what I can do to help you."

"Well, I appreciate you comin', Miss Hayes," Lacy drawled, "and I can sure use some help!"

Hayes noticed a collection of papers spread across the side table at which Lacy sat. A large magnifying glass rested on top of the papers; the glass betrayed Lacy's vision impairment, which he otherwise tired to minimize.

"What kind of help do you need, Mr. Lacy?" Hayes asked

"I could really use some food. The hospital gave me some food when I first move in here, but I ran out. I'm really hungry! The woman who brought me here said I'd be able to get a nicer motel than this, though!"

"I can get you some food in a few minutes," replied Hayes. "I don't know who brought you here, but this is the only motel available to you. Before I get you some food, I wanted to talk about your situation, how you ended up here."

"Well, I jest don't understand it, ma'am," Lacy drawled. "I'm supposed to get some money from my bank, jest like I do every week. It hasn't come this week. I've been tryin' to call my bank, and they keep sayin' they're gonna look into it, but I haven't gotten a call back."

"What bank is this money in?" Hayes asked, trying to get some information.

Lacy looked at her cautiously and answered, "I don't believe I ought to tell you that."

"Well, where did this money come from?" Hayes continued to probe.

"I'm not sure I can tell you that either," Lacy mutted. "I don't wanna get in any trouble with the government, and I don't wanna give you any information that might keep me from getting my money."

"It sounds to me you may have run out of money," Hayes suggested. "The woman at the motel where you were living said you simply stopped paying your daily bill, after almost a year and a half."

"Yeah…"

"Were you getting some kind of social security or pension or something?"

"No", he said, "I don't want no government aid."

"Did you work?"

"Yeah, I was a barber."

"How many years were you a barber?"

"Ummm…" he thought, rubbing the back of his neck. "…probably about three years, altogether."

Hayes, who specialized in psychiatric diagnoses, tried to pin-point what Mr. Lacy's might be as she talked. Although he seemed alert, he also seemed to have trouble answering questions; it took him a while, as if he might be organically or developmentally delayed in some way.

"Did you have any other job?"

"Yeah, I worked here and there…never very long."

"So, you probably didn't earn social security. Where did you live before you came here?"

"I lived in San Diego for a while…" he replied vaguely, as if the memories were slowly returning to him, "…that's where I was a barber."

"When did you live in San Diego…"

"1958…after I got out of the army."

"Where were you in the army?

"In Florida…"

"Where did you live before you came out here?"

"I lived in Texas…then I lived in Las Vegas for a while…then I came out here?"

"Where did you live in Texas?"

"Out near San Antonio…"

"Do you have any relatives out there?"

"I have a brother named Tom…he lives out near Austin."

"When was the last time you saw or spoke to Tom?"

"It's been at least a couple of years."

"Did you get the money you had while you were living in Texas?"

Lacy began to respond, when suddenly he stopped himself. "No…I can't tell you that. Damn, I wish that damn bank would call me."

Hayes decided to bypass the subject of money – which seemed to stone wall the interview – in favor of a different approach.

"I see you have a magnifying glass," she said. "Do you have visual impairments?"

"I didn't used to, but lately my eyesight seems to be getting worse."

"When was the last time you saw a doctor?"

"The other day…when I was at the hospital…"

"What about before that?"

"It's been a long time."

"Have you seen a doctor on your own since you came out here to live?"

"No, I haven't"

"The hospital said you had no medical insurance. Is that true?"

"Yeah, well, since I don't got no doctor," Lacy reasoned slowly, "I don't really need medical insurance, now do I?"

"Have you ever applied for Medicaid or Medi-Cal?"

"Naw…like I said, I don't want no government assistance. All I need is my money, and when I get it, every thing will be fine."

What do you plan to do when you get your money?"

"I'll find myself another place to live, of course."

"Do you know this area? Do you know where to look to find another place to live?"

"Well, not really…but it'll work out, some how."

"What happens if no more money comes?

"That won't happen," he stated emphatically, becoming impatient with the questioning. "The bank is supposed to send me money".

"Okay, but let's just say, what if the money doesn't come?"

"Well, I don't know," Lacy pondered, as if unwilling to even consider the possibility. 'You know, I even wrote to the President, asking him to help me get my money. I have a copy of the letter here."

"The president of the bank?"

"No, President Obama, the President of the United States."

"Can I see the letter?"

Lacy ran his fingers along the papers in front of him, and finally pulled out a white sheet with purple felt writing on it. He examined it with the magnifying glass, and then handed it to the social worker. She read it:

Dear President Obama:

I need your help. I have been receiving my income from a bank account with the Bank of the Pacific in Maple Creek. But, they are no longer sending my money, and they won't return my phone call.

I am a veteran, and now I am asking you, as President of the United States, to help me get my money back. Please call them or write to them, and tell them to do their job. I voted for you in the last election, and I am a full supporter of you as President.

Thank you.

James William Lacy

Hayes glanced up slowly from the letter, making a mental note of the bank's name. As she considered its implications, she marveled at the childlike quality of the letter: Lacy actually believed the President of the United States would intervene to affect his solitary banking account. Lacy lived in a world of his own, with his own version of reality, and possibility.

"What are you hoping President Obama will do for you?"

"Why, make the bank give me my money, of course," Lacy replied, incredulously.

"Are you sure Obama will write to you?"

"Of course…he wrote to me before." Lacy pulled a form letter from his pile, complete with the Presidential seal on it. Lacy had clearly written to the President several times; but it was also clear that these formulated, generic replies had been the only responses he'd ever received. Hayes could not tell whether Lacy simply did not realize because of his visual difficulties, or whether he simply believed what he wanted to believe.

Hayes studied the elderly man for a moment. Clearly, this man had run out of whatever source of money he had – perhaps an inheritance of some sort – but somehow had not been able to anticipate when he would run out of money. Or perhaps, consistent with his pattern, he simply would not allow himself to believe he would ever run out of money, because he knew he would never be able to earn that kind of money again. Hayes theorized a cognitive disability as well as delusional thinking; he seemed incapable of keeping track of his finances, and he could believe the President of the United States would personally intervene on his behalf. Still, he managed to live on his own for a year and a half. The mysterious Mr. Lacy presented a whole plethora of puzzles.

"Mr. Lacy," Hayes said, "we're going to have to develop a contingency plan, in case this money of yours doesn't show up."

"No," Lacy insisted, "I don't wanna talk about this no more. I ain't gonna think negatively about this. I know my money's gonna come to me, and I know the President is gonna help me! I don't wanna talk about this anymore!"

Hayes decided to postpone any further questioning. She figured she could find out whatever else she needed to know from the bank in Maple Creek. Obviously, Mr. Lacy's obstinacy made further inquiry impossible for the moment. Perhaps, she hoped, if given a few days, he might come to the realization that is money is not coming.

"I'll tell you what, Mr. Lacy," Hayes said. "I'll put you up for the remainder of the weekend on the condition if the money does not get to you by Monday afternoon, you agree to tell me more about your situation, and let me work with you to find another source of income, and another place to live."

"But I know my money will come."

"Okay, Mr. Lacy. But just in case it doesn't, do you agree to my terms?"

"Well, all right, but I know it won't be necessary. I just have to think positively.

"Okay, Mr. Lacy. I'm going to get you some food, and then I'll be back."

"Well, I appreciate it. I sure am hungry."

Six days later, the APS unit assembled in Room B for its weekly Thursday morning staff meeting. The meeting offered the unit an opportunity to air concerns, convey information on division-wide developments, and discuss issues pertinent to the profession. The meetings often featured speakers from programs and organizations, whose work is pertinent to the issues Adult Protective Services workers face. Often garnished by a tempting assortment of pastries, bagels, and beverages, the unit meeting also gave the staff an informal opportunity to spend time with one another.

The presence of quantities of sweet rolls and juices – and for that matter, any other kind of edible delicacy – was a common phenomenon at Adult Services. It seemed to be a well known fact that a plate of cake, cookies, candy – placed anywhere within the confines of a human services workplace – will have its contents disappear within a matter of a few short minutes. Even in an office virtually empty of personnel, those personnel will suddenly materialize, as if possessing an innate sugar detection system. Workers will suddenly return from the field, adjourn important meetings, end interview while the goodies quietly – almost imperceptibly – disappear. The presence of a significant number of portly individuals suggested a certain interdependence between blood sugar levels and social work performance levels.

In any case, as the APS staff shared the repast, Chuck Corley opened the meeting with announcements, and then invited individual staff members to share whatever issue seemed pertinent to the moment. Bob Foster, sitting at the opposite head of the rectangular table from Corley, spoke right up.

"Yeah, I have something," Foster said sternly, holding up a copy of a memo which had recently circulated through the office.

"This memo, from the health director, requesting we refrain from parking our cars in the street; Is she kidding?"

"What do you mean?" Corley calmly inquired.

"I mean, how can she regulate where we part outside the county plant. I've been living in this city for ten years, and as a resident I have the right to park on the public streets as much as any other resident, and she don't have much to say about it. Don't she have anything else to worry about?"

"Apparently, some of the neighbors around the campus have been complaining," Corley explained. "They would prefer county workers park in county parking lots."

"Excuse me, Chuck," interjected Emma Hayes, sitting two seats from Corley's left, "but there's never enough room in the parking lot, especially if you arrive late. There's no where else to park but on the street."

"I understand," Corley responded, "but you are being expected to comply with the request as much as possible."

"Well, I'm sorry…" Foster continued. "But I resent the presumption on the part of the health director that she can tell me where to park my car. She has absolutely no jurisdiction over this…"

"I'm afraid she does," Corley responded in his quiet, firm way.

"How..?" Foster pushed the issue. Corley started to respond when Sollie Rivers – sitting directly to Corley's right – veered the topic. "Whatever happened to the alternative parking that they were going to provide?"

"It's still in the works," Corley said. "They were going to make an arrangement with a local shopping center to set aside some spaces for county employees. They also planned to run a shuttle from that parking lot to the county building. But as yet, it hasn't happened."

"Be that as it may…" Foster said.

"Look, all I can say," Corley continued, "is the request has been made by the Director of the Health Department. It's up to you to comply in the best way you can."

The unit mumbled for a bit more, and then quiet descended upon the meeting.

"Anything else anyone wants to bring up for discussion?"

There were no volunteers.

"Okay," the supervisor said, glancing into his black notebook, "then today I want to spend a half hour or so talking about security, how safe you feel doing your jobs. You all often find yourselves in rather volatile situations, under very trying circumstances and hostile environments. It's important to me that you feel as safe as possible under those circumstances. Obviously, we are not all as big as Bob," Corley said, gesturing toward the six-foot, five inch social worker at the other end of the table, as the rest of the unit grinned. "And unlike cops, we do not carry weapons. So, I'd like to hear your feelings on the subject: do you feel safe on your job? How do you cope with how you feel? What could you do – what could we all do – to help you feel more secure?"

The meeting once again fell silent, as each person settled into personal thoughts and feelings regarding the subject. The spectra of personal risk had confronted them each at one time or another; each social worker and each public health nurse has had to reconcile the issue of personal safety, knowing it to be part and parcel to the career each had chosen. Risk is part of the territory; and while it is something about which nobody enjoyed thinking, Corley deemed it important enough to revisit now and again.

"I don't know," Sollie Rivers spoke up, per his inclination. Rivers, especially, seemed to excel at taking risks, and breaking the ice. "I've gotten into some pretty intense situations. I've had the door slammed in my face, and I was threatened on the front porch by Mrs. Giaganti's son-in-law. Most of the time it isn't a problem, but every once in a while it comes up – usually when I don't expect it," Rivers said, reflecting inward. "That's when it's scary."

"For me, it's the neighborhoods I get into, "Emma Hayes added, "like areas of Rogers Park, Dalton City, and Richland. There are certain places I will not go to after three pm, and certain places I will not go to by myself."

"And there's the dogs," Rhonda Pagan chimed in. "I was in one house in Meyersdale where this huge rottweiler suddenly jumped out of nowhere as I was opening the front gate. I was lucky I didn't open it all the way, or I might have been trapped in there with it."

"I heard there was one situation where some cop in Ashland actually shot a dog," said Foster. "He and his partner were trying to approach the house, and this big dog attacked, so the cop had to shoot it."

The staff snickered nervously a bit, but each knew the reality of the situation. The group quieted down again.

"If I get any inclination from the referral that there is any physical danger present, or even the hint of physical danger," Brennan said, "I'll ask a police officer to accompany me. I don't have many standards, but my one rule is: Don't wrestle the clients – basic social work 101."

The group giggled. "Good advice, Patrick," Pagan laughed.

"Oh, yeah," Foster said, "as big as I may be, I ain't wrestlin' clients either. One of us is gonna get hurt. A lot of times, I find just having the cop there keeps any escalation from occurring in the first place."

"That's true," said Hayes, "but sometimes having a cop there suppresses the situation. Sometimes client and families won't be as open with what is going on with the police standing in their front room"

"It can be a tough balance," Rivers added.

"What if you accompanied each other?" Corley suggested. "If you want someone to go with you, but don't necessarily want to take the police, why not ask one of your colleagues to go?"

The staff looked about at each other, nodding. "That's a good idea," Hayes said. "I've thought about that before, asking Patrick or Sollie to go, but everybody's so busy."

"If I can work it, I'd go," said Rivers

"Me too," said Brennan.

Everyone else around the table agreed.

"It's true that everyone is busy here," Corley added. "We tend to think we don't have the luxury of asking each other to do extra things. But it's most important that we all feel safe in what we do, or we can't be very effective in our work. Fear zaps us of our skills as well as our confidence. If you would like one of your colleagues to accompany you, let me know, and I will help to adjust your schedules to fit it in."

More nods circled the table. "Good idea," Rivers spoke for the group.

"Well, good," Corley said. "We need to wrap this meeting up, but I would like to return to this topic again at some time. And, of course, if any of you would like to discuss it further with me at any time, please do not hesitate. It is very important."

More nods.

"Okay, thanks," Corley concluded, as he arose from the meeting table. The rest of the staff followed, and soon the conference room was clear.

Later that day Sandra, the young receptionist at Adult Services, wandered up to the desk of Donna Briar, seated updating her call log. "Excuse me, Donna", the receptionist said.

"Yes" Briar responded.

"We have a drop in named Priscilla Stone," Sandra said. "She says she's homeless and she can't get any help from anyone."

"Priscilla Stone…" Briar ruminated "…why does that name sound familiar?"

"She's been here before," Sandra informed her. "Both Bob and Patrick have dealt with her. She's short, with short hair, and a terrycloth robe and sandals…"

"Oh, yeah…" Briar told her, "…tell her I'll be out in a minute."

Donna Briar immediately searched for Priscilla Stone's name in the mental health database. It revealed numerous contacts with various components of the mental health system, including Psychiatric Emergency. Her last contact seemed to have been with the Mobile Crisis Team (MCT)

The Mobile Crisis Team, a non-profit mental health agency, specialized in working with the mentally ill indigent. The MCT would go out to the streets, or to shelters, or under bridges; wherever a homeless mentally ill person might be. They would work with the mentally disabled adults under 65, who normally have no other physical impairments.

Dialing the MCT number, Briar spoke with an old acquaintance, Ivan Anderson, whom Briar had known when she worked at the developmentally disabled center. Anderson had been the Crisis Team director for many years; APS and MCT had developed a mutual understanding, and often referred clients between them.

Anderson informed Briar that Stone's situation remained the same: she had been referred to several residential facilities for the mentally impaired, but she had always chosen to walk away from them. Like many with a psychiatric impairment, Stone assumed the problem lay in the world and the people that inhabited it, and not in herself. Stone's option at the moment, Anderson said, was to voluntarily take herself to the Mental Health office in Cedarwood City, and allow herself to be evaluated for the proper dose of medications. If she remained unwilling to do so, neither the MCT nor county Mental Health would offer her anything else.

As soon as Briar saw Priscilla Stone, she immediately recalled descriptions Brennan and Foster had given of the encounters with her. Briar also recalled seeing her on the streets of Cedarwood several times – in all types of weather – wandering about, waiting for a bus, or standing on a street concern. She stood short in stature – maybe shorter than Briar at 5"0". She always dressed in a terry-cloth robe which barely reached to mid-thigh. She wore light rubber thongs on her feet, and wore plastic sandwich bags on her hands.

Briar greeted Stone in the lobby, and led her to an interview room. Briar sat down at the interview table, but Stone would not, preferring to stand away from the table. She tugged at her robe with her hands wrapped in plastic baggies. She relayed her story to the social worker: she does not want to go to the mental health clinic, because they will give her medications that make her drowsy. She said she is staying with a roommate right now, but lately they have not been getting along, and she wants another place to stay. Briar informed her that living on SSI as she did, she does not have many options. The best thing to do, she advised, would be to patch things up with her roommate, and to seek treatment at county mental health.

"Who told you I should seek treatment?" Stone demanded.

"I spoke to Ivan Anderson at the Mobile Crisis Team."

"Oh, that man," Stone complained, "he acts as if he's my case manager, but he's not. I don't have to do what he says."

"Well, you do if you want another living arrangement," Briar said. "If you don't comply with the mental health treatment prescribed, nobody is going to help you further."

"That's terrible!" Stone said. "Nobody will help me!" As Stone complained, pacing about the room, looking out the window, Briar watched her in her highly unusual attire. Unable to restrain herself further, Briar simply had to ask.

"Are you in need of some clothing?" she asked. "Aren't you cold?"

"On, no," Stone answered, "I thought you knew. This is the only thing I can wear that doesn't irritate my skin. If I wear anything else, it itches terribly, and I am very uncomfortable."

"I see," said Briar. "Is it a problem with your skin? Have you seen a dermatologist?"

"Oh, yeah, I've seen several dermatologists, but they all say there's nothing wrong with me. They never see a rash, and they can never figure out the problem. I don't understand it! These doctors are nuts!"

"Do you have a problem with your hands as well?" Briar continued to probe, watching Stone's fingers through the plastic cellophane.

"I'm afraid of catching diseases," Stone said. "Everything is so dirty, and there are so many bugs out there. I just can't take the chance that I'll catch anything. This is the best way to protect myself."

"I see," Briar said.

"So, are you going to help me? Please? I need another place to stay."

"I'm sorry, Ms. Stone," Briar said. "I told you how you can help yourself!"

"But I can't do that! You don't understand!" Stone demanded. "Those medicines make me sick. I can't do what they want me to. Please! Please!"

"Well, since you are already open to mental health, we are not going to open a second case. Your option is to go back to mental health or the crisis team, and let them help you. If you don't like what they do, then talk to the patient advocate."

"They're no good either! They just tell me to do what Ivan Anderson wants me to do."

"I'm sorry," Briar said, standing up at the table. For once, Briar stood taller than another adult human being. "You're going to have to go now."

"No, please," Stone argued vehemently. But still, Briar managed to guide her out the door, and back into the lobby. Stone argued further, even as Briar closed the door behind her. Finally, realizing she would get nowhere, Stone left, as the March rain continued to fall outside.

The following Monday, Emma Hayes caught up to Patrick Brennan in the break room at the Adult Services office. She told him about James Lacy, and her encounters with him. After allowing him to stay at the Wayside Inn over the weekend, despite Lacy's assurances to the contrary, he again refused to provide Hayes information, and refused to cooperate in Hayes' efforts to find him a source to income and a home.

"He simply can't or won't get beyond the belief that his money is simply delayed somehow, and not used up," Hayes exclaimed. "He doesn't trust the government anyway – for reasons I can't possibly understand – and he won't do anything he believes will jeopardize the delivery of his money."

"I'd heard about the case through Donna," Brennan said. "Did we ever figure out exactly what his source of money is?"

"Not really; I wasn't able to find any relatives in Texas, Arizona, or anywhere else, but my guess is the money was an inheritance of some kind. How else could he have received an apparently large sum of money with very little trace to it? He mentioned he had an aunt who had died; from my estimation, to live as he did for the last two years, it would have taken about $80,000. My guess is he spent it all, but doesn't have the capacity to figure out that he has run out of money. I contacted the bank officer in Maple Creek. As you know, bank personnel are very reluctant to give out information about their customers. Although the officer wouldn't tell me how much Lacy's account once was, he did tell me Lacy no longer holds an account at the bank."

"So…" Brennan said, anticipating the scenario Hayes was about to present.

"So, he won't cooperate with any plan I set for him. He wants Adult Services to continue to pay the bill at the Wayside Inn – in fact, he actually wants me to place him at a nicer hotel – but he doesn't' want to work with me to apply for SSI, or a board and care or anything else. He is the strangest man I've ever met. He keeps insisting I think positively, and he is unwavering in his belief that one day the President is going to swoop down from the sky and rescue him. For whatever reason – and I cannot figure our why – he cannot bring himself to understand his current situation, and figure out a plan for providing for himself.

"So, he has to go, huh?" Brennan surmised reluctantly.

"I'm afraid so; his time at the motel is up tomorrow at eleven. I won't be at work tomorrow, so I was wondering if you could go to the motel and place him on a hold. I hate to do this, because he certainly does not need a hospital, but I don't know what else to do. I don't want to extend the motel time, because that will just feed into his delusion and dependence, and he will probably renege afterwards anyway. Unless Lacy's attitude and capabilities alter quickly, I think he's going to need a conservator. He definitely needs an evaluation to determine what his diagnosis and treatment – if any –would be."

"Too bad for you you're off tomorrow," Brennan quipped.

"Oh, yeah…I'm crushed," Hayes said, "You know how much I love doing psychiatric holds."

'Okay," Brennan said, placing a hand on her shoulder. "I'll see if a car's available tomorrow."

"Thanks, Patrick."

The next day, under a cloudy sky, Patrick Brennan's white Tempo pulled into the parking lot of the Wayside Inn. Brennan crossed the parking lot, heading for Room 16. Knocking on the door, he had to wait several moments before the door opened. "Can I help you?" a corpulent, red-faced older man asked.

"Yes, Mr. Lacy, my name is Patrick Brennan. I work with Emma Hayes. She couldn't be here today, but she wanted me to come by and see how you're doing."

"I'm fine," he said. "I'm jest waitin' for my money. I wish it would get here soon."

"Yeah, Emma told me about that," Brennan said. "Have you heard anything else from the bank?"

"No, not yet; I jest can't understand it!"

"Can I come in, Mr. Lacy?"

Lacy shuffled backward, moving slowly, like a man accustomed to doing everything slowly. He groped ahead of himself for the edge of the bed, where he sat with a heavy sigh. His eyesight appeared to be even worse than Emma Hayes had described. Brennan glanced about the room, which was still fairly neat, but had the lived-in look. It was warm and muggy inside. Bread wrappers and luncheon meat containers rested on the dresser. Two bottles of water lay sideways on the carpet next to the dresser.

"How y' feelin'? Brennan asked him.

"Oh, okay. My back hurts a little…"

"You sound a little out of breath. Are you okay?"

"Yeah, I'm all right," Lacy sighed this magnifying glass," he said, pointing in the general direction of the side table.

Brennan placed his hands on his hips, surveying the scene for a few moments.

"Well, you know, Mr. Lacy, you can't stay in this motel anymore. The county has only paid for you through today, and you can't stay here any longer."

"I can't leave. The bank's going to call me!"

"The bank is not gonna call you, Mr. Lacy. You have no more money in your account. We checked with the bank, and your account is closed. We need to figure out what to do with you, because you can't stay here."

"I was under the impression that ya'll were gonna find me another motel."

"I'm sorry, Mr. Lacy. You are under a mistaken impression. Now, are you interested in working with Ms. Hayes, to find another way to support yourself?"

"I can't leave, I told you that," Lacy vehemently stated, growing angry. "The President is going to help me. I wrote to him. I'll get my money, and I'll find another place to live."

"Mr. Lacy, you can't even find your way around this room. Even if you have the money, how could you possibly find yourself another place to live.

"I'd call a taxi, to take me around to the motels."

"Mr. Lacy, you can't call a taxi. You have no more money."

Lacy, paused, as if suddenly realizing the dire nature of the situation, but then returned to his familiar pattern. "Well, then, I'll jest have to wait here for the bank to call!"

Brennan realized there was no way he was going to be able to convince Lacy of the truth. He would simply have to act. "Okay, Mr. Lacy, I'm going to leave now. Are you sure you don't want Ms. Hayes to help you?"

"No, thank you. But you tell her I sure do appreciate her efforts. But I'm going to stay right here."

"Okay…" Brennan ended, as he closed the motel door behind him.

Patrick Brennan saw no wisdom in making ultimatums, or alert the potential psychiatric hold patients too soon about the impending destinations. Over the years he found the less time there was to think about things, the less anxious they became; the less chance they had to become reactive, and the easier it was to get them into the ambulance.

The course was clear. James Lacy would have to go to the hospital against his will. He could not devise a reasonable plan for obtaining his food, clothing, and shelter, the very definition of "gravely disabled adult." He had no money to support himself – although he arduously believed he could – and he refused to apply for public assistance. He apparently could not accept reality that the leisure and contentment of the last eighteen months – however it came to him – would never be again. His delusion – coupled with his visual impairment – made it impossible for him to take care of himself. He would be taken to the county hospital for an evaluation, to verify Emma Hayes belief that Lacy needed a conservator.

Brennan returned to his car. He called Psychiatric Emergency Services, advised them of the situation, and asked them to send an ambulance to the Wayside Inn. Then he called the Cedarwood Police Department for an officer standby. Although he felt it unlikely Lacy would actually become aggressive – it seemed contrary to his nature – his bulk might make it difficult to maneuver him out of the motel room. Brennan discovered long ago the presence of a uniformed officer normally quelled whatever volatility existed, before he had a chance to escalate.

"This is the part I bloody well hate," Brennan mumbled to himself, "waiting!" He recalled the time he and Sollie Rivers had gone to the home of a wealthy but ditzy spinster to place her on a hold, and ended up waiting two hours for the ambulance to arrive. He dearly hoped this would not be such a case as well.

After nearly thirty minutes, the ambulance van rolled into the parking lot. A large-boned male and a tall woman rode in the front. A squad car from the Cedarwood City Police Department quickly followed the paramedics. Brennan quickly explained the situation to everyone, and one of the officers – named Bridges – briefly ducked into the motel manager's office, to verify the situation himself. As the group approached Room 16, Officer Bridges pushed the door open.

"Mr. Lacy?" he called.

Lacy squinted toward the door, shading his eyes with his hand, trying to discern exactly who was calling this time. "Yes," Lacy Answered."

"I'm Officer Bridges of the Cedarwood Police Department. I'm afraid I'm gong to have to ask you to vacate the premises."

"I can't, officer. I have no money. I'm waiting for my bank to call me, and send me some more money."

"The social worker says you don't have any more money. He says he has been trying to help you get some assistance and a place to live, but you won't let him.

"I can't. President Obama is supposed to contact my bank, and get my money for me."

Bridges looked at his partner, and glanced back at Brennan, who shrugged.

"Mr. Lacy, I'm afraid you're going to have to go with these paramedics to the hospital," Bridges continued.

"They're gonna take good care of you, Mr. Lacy," Brennan interjected. "A doctor's gonna give you an examination, and determine if there's anything wrong with you besides your vision. You can't stay here, Mr. Lacy, and it's not safe for you to be on the street. You can't take care of yourself, and you've no means of providing your own food, clothing, and shelter."

"I don't want to go to the hospital," Lacy protested. "I don't need the hospital."

"I'm afraid there is no choice," the policeman told him.

"I can't believe it," Lacy complained. "Why don't you jest take me to a nicer motel."

"Come on, Mr. Lacy," Bridges continued. "You go out with these paramedics."

"Can't I go to the bathroom first?"

"Sure," Bridges said, "but you have to leave the door open a little. I don't want you locking yourself in there."

The officers, the paramedics, and the social worker watched as Lacy hoisted his heavy body off the bed, and lumbered into the bathroom. He nearly walked into the wall beside the bathroom door, and then fumbled with his hands to find the doorway. He stumbled into the bathroom, closing the door partway behind him.

"How the hell did he think he'd be able to make it on his own," Bridges asked Brennan.

"That's the problem," said Brennan. "Mr. Lacy just isn't very realistic about what he can and can't do."

After Lacy finished relieving himself, the paramedics escorted him and his belongings into the ambulance van, without incident. Brennan handed the woman the psychiatric hold form, and the vehicle sped off toward the hospital.

"Thank you, officer," Brennan said politely.

"Sure thing," Bridges responded. "That was easy enough."

Back at the office, Rhonda Pagan typed a letter on the word processor while Sollie Rivers – whose cubicle shared a baffle with the nurse – spoke on the phone. His conversation seemed to grow more animated, until it apparently came to a sudden stop. Rivers whisked his headset off his ear, and cursed loud enough for Pagan to hear.

"Damned nurses!" Rivers growled.

"I resent that," Pagan called playfully over her shoulder.

"Oh...I'm sorry", Rivers mumbled, wheeling to face his colleague. "...nothing personal."

Pagan wheeled in her chair as well. "What's wrong with the damned nurses today?"

"Not all nurses," Rivers quickly retracted. "In fact, public health nurses never seem to react the way these home health nurses do...man..."

"What happened?" Pagan asked, pulling her chair closer.

"Oh, my client...he's a gruff old codger who swears the way you and I breathe. Well, he swore at the nurse who when out to see him, and now she's saying he's non-compliant. I know if she just ignored what he said, she could get him to cooperate, but it's like she's just looking for a reason to drop him."

"And the old man's giving her one."

"Yep," Rivers said, "it's like the old man understands her better than she understands him."

"Well…" Pagan shrugged. "I guess we can't all be public health nurses."

"I guess not," Rivers said. "What is it about you PHN's anyway? Why are you so different from other nurses?"

"Good looks…charm…intelligence…" Pagan smiled playfully, "you pick…"

"Well…" Rivers leaned forward, "at least in your case…"

Pagan blushed and stammered slightly. "Oh, Sollie…seriously, I think home health nurses simply are not exposed to the number and variety of people and situations, the way PHN's are. I think they are simply not prepared to deal with them."

"So, the good looks, charm, and intelligence don't apply to public health nurses."

"Maybe not," Pagan said, "but we're all angels. Haven't you seen the sign?"

Pagan pointed to a small poster card on her baffle, featuring the sketch of an angel in a nurse's outfit. The caption read:

Angels are often disguised as Public Health Nurses.

"I knew it," Rivers said. "I'm sharing a baffle with an angel."

"Don't you feel blessed?" Pagan smiled.

"I certainly do," Rivers smiled back.

On the following rainy Tuesday afternoon, Patrick Brennan drove out to the town of Plymouth, in the northwest corner of Cedarwood County. Brennan came out to interview Terrell Matthews of the well-known (to APS anyway) Matthews family. Adult Protective Services had been following the Matthews for several years, the last open case managed by Emma Hayes. Hayes became involved because Calvin Matthews - Terrell's brother – had been accused of stealing the Supplemental Security Income (SSI) check from Lucille Matthews, Terrell's mother. He would spend her check on alcohol, illicit substances, and other inappropriate expenditures. Lucille Matthews had suffered from multi-farct senile dementia, had a poor memory, and – unfortunately - trusted Calvin blindly. She willingly signed her SSI checks over to Calvin, thinking he will somehow manage the money for her benefit. The last Hayes had heard Calvin had moved his mother out of Cedarwood County, beyond the reaches of Adult Services, to apparently do as he wished with Lucille's money.

The latest referral concerning the Matthew's, however, inferred Lucille and Calvin had returned to Cedarwood County. Lucille moved in with Terrell and his girlfriend, Maggie, in their apartment in Plymouth. Even with Lucille's money, Calvin apparently could not pull it together enough to keep a permanent place to live. The last report came from the Plymouth Police Department, which reported an altercation of some type between Calvin and Terrell at Terrell's apartment. Calvin had once again taken Lucille from Terrell's apartment, bound for some unknown destination. Brennan wanted to find out from Terrell specifically what happened, and what Lucille's current situation was.

Brennan received a warm greeting at the Matthew's door. Maggie – a pleasant woman, in her late thirties; wearing a pink housecoat over some jeans – ushered Brennan quickly into the house. Terrell, on the other hand, though tall and good looking, seemed to grumble and frown a lot. He dressed in sweat suit, and wore a patch of gauze behind his right ear. He reluctantly shook the social worker's hand.

"This is where Calvin hit me," Terrell announced, even before Brennan has a chance to sit down. "He came over saying he wanted to visit my mother, and he ended up hitting me with a coke bottle on the back of my head. He took her with him."

Where'd he take her?" Brennan asked.

"I don't know," he replied. "In the past he would take her north to the city, and just drop her off somewhere. Leave her all by herself. What kind of man can do that to his own mama?"

"I don't know," Brennan commiserated. "How's your mother doing?"

"Pretty much the same," Maggie said. "She's pretty frail and forgetful. She can't manage her money at all, and can't take herself anywhere, because she'd get lost. She insists on giving her money to Calvin, who just spends it on booze and drugs or whatever."

"Yeah," Brennan said. "Emma Hayes told me she was about to refer Ms. Matthew to probate conservatorship when Calvin took her out of the state. How'd your mother end up back here?"

"Calvin got evicted for some reason," Maggie said. "He wouldn't say why. He couldn't find another apartment for him and his mother, so he brought her back here about a month ago."

"Why'd he come back last night?"

"Because he's out of money," said Maggie, "and Lucille's check comes on the fifth of the month. He came to pick up her check, and use her money. Terrell tried to stop him, and this is the result. We'll probably get some call from someone, telling us that mom has been dropped off somewhere. You just wait and see."

"When Lucille's here, does she need much assistance?"

"We take turns watching her, depending on when we're home from work. I work for the hospital, and Terrell works part-time at night as a security guard. Lucille walks okay for herself, as I said, but she gets lost. She can still feed herself, but she needs a little help getting dressed, and bathing."

"She'd be all right…" Terrell interjected grimly, "…if my brother would just leave her alone. But she thinks the world of him, and can't believe he'd ever do her wrong. I've offered to manage her money for her, but she will only let Calvin do it." More than a hint of envy tainted Terrell's voice.

"It sounds definitely like undue influence," Brennan said.

"What?" quizzed Maggie.

"Undue influence," Brennan repeated, "is essentially the sway Calvin has over your mother. Calvin uses the faith and trust your mother has in him to take advantage of her, and her money. We use this term often as a basis for a petition for conservatorship. Sometimes it's difficult to prove, because it could be argued that Mrs. Matthew is giving the money to Calvin of her own free will. In a sense she is, but we'd assert she doesn't have the mental capacity to understand the consequences of what she's doing."

"That's for sure," Terrell said.

"Our assertion's that Lucille doesn't have the capacity to protect herself against Calvin, and therefore needs a conservator to protect her money for her interest."

"I see," said Maggie. "By a conservator, you mean someone who would help Lucille?"

"A conservator's someone appointed by Superior Court to manage your mother's affairs: her money, her living arrangement, to make medical decisions, that sort of thing. The judge makes the decision based on the petition presented, and the report from the patient's doctor."

"This is something the county would do?" she asked.

"It depends," Brennan explained. "Is that something you, as her closest relatives, would be able to take on?"

"I don't know," said Maggie. "What would we have to do?"

"To become a private conservator, you yourself would have to file a petition in Superior Court most likely with the help of a lawyer. If the judge approves your petition, you'd be appointed as Lucille's conservator. You'd be in charge of paying for your mother's needs with her money."

"But I'd still have to deal with my brother, right?" Terrell asked.

"Big time," said Brennan, "You'd be in charge of making sure he didn't get your mother's money."

"And hiring a lawyer could take some money."

"Yeah, it could cost you in the thousands of dollars, and your mother – as well as your brother – would have a right to challenge the petition."

Terrell winced as he rubbed the back of his head, which was still sore from the incident the previous night. "No, thanks, man…" he said, nearly shaking with anger. "I don't need more bottles broken over my head. My brother is crazy, man! There's no tellin' what he might do."

"Well, then…" continued Brennan, "the county would conduct an investigation and, if deemed necessary – and I think it would be – would petition the court to become her conservator, of both person and estate."

"Then, that's what you should do," Terrell emphasized. "Someone needs to keep him away from my mother and her money."

"Have you and your brother had troubles in the past?" Brennan quizzed.

"They've fought all their lives, "Maggie interjected as Terrell grimaced, almost holding back tears. "Lucille has always sided with Calvin, although Terry has always treated her much better than Calvin has. Calvin just uses her, and then drops her off until he needs her again. Someone's got to protect her."

"Well, first of all…we need to find her," the social worker reminded them.

"That's right," said Maggie.

Brennan handed his card to both Maggie and Terrell. "If you hear from your mother or your brother, would you let me know?"

"Sure."

"If we find your mother, do you feel like you can still take care of her here?" Brennan continued.

Terrell stopped for a minute, and then said, "It ain't good for my mom to be with either my brother or me. If she stays here, she's gonna be in the middle of the fights between Calvin and me. Plus she always wants to be with him anyway.

Maggie continued, "We've talked about this earlier. I don't think it's safe for any of us for Lucille to be here," she said.

Patrick Brennan glanced at the gauze on Terrell's head, and nodded, "It would seem so. As soon as we make contact with her, we'll place her on a hold and arrange for her to live somewhere else. In the meantime, we will start the investigation for probate conservatorship."

As soon as he returned to the office, Brennan consulted with Emma Hayes on the Matthew's case. They sat in one of the small interview rooms at the front of the Big Room, near Chuck Corley's office, going over some of Hayes' notes.

Hayes said she remembered Calvin taking Lucille out of the county, up north to cash her check and then left her in a dangerous section of town. Hayes characterized Calvin as a "volatile con man" who used crack and alcohol, and who had numerous law enforcement entanglements. Hayes believed Lucille to be severely at risk, not due to any physical abuse on Calvin's part – there had been no such record – but due to the undue influence, the abandonment, neglect, and fiduciary abuse.

"The amazing thing is," Hayes said, "that through all Calvin does to her, Lucille never has anything bad to say about her son. Maggie told me before Calvin is almost the spitting image of his father, who died several years ago. I sometimes wonder if Lucille – in her dementia – sometimes confuses the two. Anyway, for whatever reason, Calvin and Terry have a serious sibling rivalry, which catches Lucille right in the middle."

"What do you think should be done?" asked Brennan.

"We were going to file for conservatorship when I had the case, but we could never make contact with Lucille long enough to make the move. What we need is to be able to hold onto Lucille long enough to file for temporary conservatorship, which will gives us temporary authority over her. Unfortunately, there's nothing we can do until we find out where Lucille is."

Brennan said, "I hope Calvin doesn't drop her off someplace where she can really get hurt."

Chapter 4
APRIL

James Lacy languished in the psychiatric ward while psychiatrists and psychiatric nurses attempted to diagnose his condition. Physically, he had hypertension and obesity. Nearly blind, his eyes had contracted cataracts which had never been treated. Mentally, he remained alert and oriented, but continued to cling to his specific delusions: Money remained in his bank; President Obama would intervene in his financial difficulties; discussing the situation with others would jeopardize the return of his funds. Throughout his stay, Lacy refused to cooperate with interviews, refused to agree to medical examinations, essentially refused to allow any investigation into his mysterious past.

Finally after about a month in the hospital, with precious little more discovered about him, the best diagnosis devised by psychiatrists became "Delusional Disorder." This means little more than he experiences delusions. With no alternative – and with hospital discharge planners balking at keeping him longer – the psychiatric ward referred James Lacy to the Public Guardian for a probate conservator. His fixed delusion – more than any physical impairment - made him a gravely disabled adult.

After the court granted conservatorship, the assigned deputy public guardian applied for public assistance for him, placing him in a small residential care facility, for which public assistance paid. He lived rather contently and politely – as per his way – still able to dress himself, bathe himself, and feed himself, albeit still very slowly, But he never shook the believe that substantial money would still come to him and somehow – someday – the President of the United States would rescue him from his plight.

On a sunny April Friday afternoon, in the town of Dalton City, a white county Tempo parked against the curb in a low-income neighborhood. As he and Rhonda Pagan climbed inside, Sollie River asked, "So, what do you think?"

"Well, she definitely has some congestion in hr lungs," Pagan suggested. "It could develop into pneumonia if she isn't careful."

"I hope you scared her into compliance," Rivers said, as he steered the county car away from the curb. "She has plenty of money, and a good health plan, and no other medical complaints, but she hates going to the doctor."

"A lot of women her age do," said Pagan. "But, she agreed to go, and the attendant that made the referral is certainly willing to take her. If she had to pay for a cab or something, she would never go."

"She might not go anyway," said Rivers. "We'll have to wait and see..."

"What if she doesn't?"

"I don't know," Rivers said. "It would be pretty tough to conserve her simply because she hates doctors – especially since she hasn't seen one in twenty years, and it hasn't done her much harm up until now. Hopefully, we've bluffed her into going this time."

"Yeah, hopefully," agreed Pagan.

"Wasn't it cute how she talked about her wedding, and showed us that picture of her and her husband. She sure seems to miss him."

Pagan did not respond. She sat quietly, her head slightly bowed, Rivers glanced over at her. "Rhonda, are you okay?"

Pagan bowed her head even lower. A lone tear rolled down her cheek. "It's off, Sollie."

"What's off, Rhonda?" Rivers said. He thought for a minute, and then gasped, "Oh, my God...the wedding? The wedding's off?"

"Yeah," Pagan sniffed, "we're not getting married. You were right, Sollie. I should've gotten it in writing!"

"Oh, my God, Rhonda," Rivers said again. "I'm sorry...I never should have said that. I can't believe this!" Rivers placed a sympathetic hand on the nurse's shoulder. "When did this happen?"

"We called it off more than a week ago," she said. "There were just too many fights between our families...especially me and his family."

"I'm so sorry, Rhonda," he said.

"He couldn't choose between me and his family. He was so wrapped up in them…and his expectations about the wedding…our life…that I couldn't go through with it. He wasn't willing to be flexible…about anything…"

"Oh, Rhonda…I'm so sorry…," Rivers said, taking her into his arms. He cradled her head on his shoulder, as her hand stroked his brown pony tail while she cried softly."

"Oh, Sollie," she said. "I'm so lucky we sit next to each other. You've been such a good friend to me. You help me to forget all about this…"

"Well, whatever I can do for you," Rivers said. "Who knows? Maybe it's for the best."

Sollie and Rhonda held each other tightly some more. Pagan looked up into Rivers' green eyes. "Maybe you're right," she said. They gazed deeply at each other for a moment, and then – seemingly out of nowhere – Rhonda reached her lips up to Sollie's. A special energy seemed to erupt as their lips met, in what developed into a deep, passionate and prolonged kiss.

Several days later, Donna Briar wheeled her chair toward the two other phone workers and Sollie Rivers, who sat beside them. "So, are you guys going to bring me some baked goods for the spring boutique on Thursday?"

"Me?" chirped Foster. "You want me to bake?"

The men chuckled. "You don't have to actually bake," said Briar. "You can just buy something at the bakery that you could donate to the boutique."

More giggling followed.

"Let's see," Brennan said. "I'm trying to think of a bakery I can stop at on my bicycle on my way to work. I'll just cram the stuff from the bakery in my backpack. I'm sure it'll be all right."

"Well, just get the day-old stuff," Foster said. "I'll withstand anything."

More chuckling ensued.

"What is the boutique for again?" Foster asked.

"…for the adult fund."

"That's right," Foster said.

"What's the adult fund doing with its money these days," asked Brennan.

"You know, one time purchases, mostly. A lot of clients in long term case management or under the public guardian get microwaves."

"APS doesn't use it very much, does it?"

"No," Briar said. "Those clients seem to have more long term, chronic needs the adult fund can't handle."

"How many fundraisers does the adult fund have each year?" Foster asked.

"About four or five," Briar said.

Just then the hotline bell rang. Foster rolled his eyes. "What do you want?" he mumbled out loud, denigrating the nerve of the caller to actually dial the number. "Excuse me," he said to his colleagues. "Adult Services," Foster answered the telephone.

"This is John Butler from the Shelton Police. I think we need a social worker out here as soon as possible."

"What's the problem?"

"I'm at the First Fidelity Bank here in Shelton. Apparently an elderly man came her about an hour ago, and showed the bank officer a copy of a document that seems to suggest he is about to sell his home to a neighbor for $30,000."

"What??"

"Here….let me have you talk to the bank officer. Her name is Lelani Yee."

"Okay," Foster mumbled, as a woman picked up the other end.

"Hello," she said. "I'm Lelani Yee, and I'm the chief loan officer."

"Hello, this is Bob Foster from Adult Protective Services for the county. I understand you have a situation there."

"Yes, one of our customers, whose name is Clarence Willits, came into our bank. He is 87 years old, and he appeared very confused. He told me he wanted to take out a six thousand dollar loan to fix up his house, so that he can sell it to a neighbor for $30,000.

"How much is the house worth?"

"Probably at least $480,000, we are estimating. This house has not been worth $30,000 in probably forty years. Mr. Willits owns the house, and he could easily afford the loan, but I am very concerned about this sale."

"How long have you known this man?"

"He's been a customer here for many years. His wife died several years ago, and he has a daughter in the Midwest somewhere. Actually, one of our staff gave him a ride home once. He lives pretty close to downtown here. The staff member said the house is small, and the roof seems to be leaking a little, but it is certainly worth much more than $30,000."

"Do you know anything about his neighbor?"

"No, except Clarence says he's been helping him with his grocery shopping and other chores, and he wants to leave him the house. The problem is I'm not certain he has anywhere else to go. I'm also not sure if he has figured out what he would do for another place to live if he sold the house."

"That's not good," Foster said.

"No", Yee echoed. "Also, the document he showed me looked rather suspect. Apparently two of the witnesses to the transaction are employees of the real estate officer. One of the loan officers here has worked with the real estate agent before, and considers him very shady."

"Oh?" Foster muttered.

"I seriously wonder if Willits actually understands what he is about to do."

"I wonder that too," Foster said, jotting down some further notes on his pad.

"The police officer," Yee said, "told me you have the power to stop the sale of the house."

"Under the authority of the public guardian," Foster explained, "we have the ability to freeze or seize all of his assets and property, pending a conservatorship investigation." Foster thought for a moment, and then said, "I'm going to come out to the bank to talk some more with you about this. I'll probably be there within an hour, but first let me get some more information on Mr. Willits."

After obtaining the pertinent demographic data on Willits, Foster hurried to the office of the Probate Conservatorship Supervisor, to authorize the release of a 3701 form. This form authorized – through the probate code - the Public Guardian and its agents – in this case, Foster – to require the following cooperation from banks and other financial institutions:

Without the necessity of inquiring into the truth of this certificate and without court order or letters being issued, to:

Provide the public guardian information concerning the property held in the sole name of the estate.

Surrender to the public guardian property of the estate that is subject to loss, injury, waste, or misappropriation

Constitutes sufficient a quittance for providing information and for surrendering the property

Fully discharges the county recorder, financial institution, or other person from any liability for any act or omission of the public guardian with respect to the property.

The form carried the seal of the Public Guardian, who is also the Director of the County Health Department.

The 3701 form essentially allows the Public Guardian to protect the assets and property from theft or misappropriation, when it is suspected that the owner of the property lacks the cognitive capacity to provide that protection alone. The 3701 is issued in conjunction with and pending an investigation for the probate conservatorship. In cases of bank accounts, it prevents unauthorized withdrawals or transactions that might be perpetrated by fiscal abusers. In the case of property – such as Mr. Willits house – it circumvents any possible sale or loan against the property, with the assumption that Mr. Willits does not understand the consequences of what is being done.

It is a scary document from the point of view of the bank, which is normally forbidden to reveal anything about the financial portfolio of a customer. The phrase: "Without necessity of inquiring into the trust of the certificate and without court orders" means the bank simply must trust the word of whoever shows up in possession of this document, that the situation that he or she is presenting is indeed true. It places considerable amount of power into the hands of the bearer. In the thirty-six year history of the Public Guardian of Cedarwood County, there had been only two incidents of inappropriate use of the 3701, and both times a renegade Deputy Public Guardian used the form.

This document might be the basis of the widespread myth that county can simply move in, and take away money and property whenever it wants. The truth is the public guardian can take such steps only in conjunction with a conservatorship investigation. Normally, in the case of a temporary conservatorship, the Guardian prevents anyone else from taking the money or the property. And if the Superior Court judge decides later against the appointment of a conservator, the authority over money or property is immediately returned to the owner. If the Public Guardian is appointed as conservator, the DPG will use the authority of the court to manage the money.

The purpose of the 3701 is to protect money and property of an incapacitated individual as quickly as possible. Since the goal in those cases is to safeguard what often amount to the entire life savings of a highly vulnerable individual, the ability to act swiftly and completely is often imperative.

With the 3701 forms in hand, Foster left for the First Fidelity Bank. With no county car available, Foster hopped on his classic Harley Davidson FXDB, Dyna Glide Sturgis motorcycle. Foster dressed in leather jacket, dark glasses, and helmet over his casual shirt and pants work attire. He made his way to the main county highway, north to the town of Shelton. At the bank, Foster met Yee – a long-haired woman in a gray business suit – who provided the addresses and phone numbers of both Mrs. Willits, and the Continental Tile Company, which had drawn up the dubious document for the transfer of title. Foster handed Yee a copy of the 3701 and requested she inform him of any attempt by anyone trying to remove money from Willits' account.

Following Yee's direction, Foster drove to a business section of the small town. Tall, gleaming steel and glass buildings towered over vast parking lots filled with a variety of vehicles. Foster parked his cycle, and followed the signs to the Continental Title Company.

Riding the elevator to the fifth floor, Foster found the title company's office. In it, sitting at a desk among the carpeted floor and crowded book shelf, sat a smarmy looking secretary named Florence Schnur. She worked for an agent named Dan Fazzino. With cigarette dangling precariously from her lower lip, Schnur responded with a certain amount of surprise mixed with contempt when Foster handed her the 3701. Glaring down at her, he announced his authorization to postpone the sale of Mr. Willit's property on Baker Street until the Public Guardian could sufficiently determine the appropriateness and legality of the sale.

"How long will this investigation take?" Schnur impatiently asked.

"It's hard to say…probably a couple of weeks, at least."

"But the sale is supposed to be finalized tomorrow?"

"Exactly," Foster said. "I am sure Fazzino would not want to engage in a real estate transaction that is illegal."

"Illegal?" Schur snubbed.

"Yes, it's illegal to enter into a contract with an individual who's cognitively unable to understand the contract."

"Of course," Schnur muttered, "if only Mr. Fazzino realized. Still, he is not going to be happy with this."

"Well, if Mr. Fazzino has any concerns, he can call me directly, and I will bring him up to speed." Foster reached way down and handed Ms. Schnur his card. "By the way, do you know who was present when this deal was negotiated?"

"Well, there was Mr. Fazzino, myself, Mr. Willits, the neighbor, the neighbor's real estate agent, and a couple of women with the agent."

"Is this the name of the neighbor's real estate agent?" Foster showed her the document.

"Yes, that's him, Jay King."

"Do you know who these other signatures belong to? These witnesses..?"

Schnur peered for a moment, and then deciphered, "They belong to the women, who signed as witnesses."

"Do you know who the women are?"

"I think they work with him, or for him, or something?"

"Employees of the real estate agent are acting as witnesses to the deal?"

"I don't…know," Schnur hesitated.

"Did Mr. Willits have any representation with him?"

"No. He came in with the neighbor."

"So the man to whom he was going to sell the home at such a ridiculous price drove him to the transaction meeting?"

"Uh, yeah…? But Mr. Willits seemed in agreement of the deal."

"Really…" Foster peered down, "we have some serious question as to whether Mr. Willits had the capacity to make this decision, and whether his neighbor had taken serious advantage of him. Before we allow this deal to go forward, we need to make sure he understands the consequences of the deal, and how that might affect his future ability to care for himself."

"Okay," Schnur said. "I will give Mr. Fazzino the message."

"Thank you," said Foster. "I would appreciate it."

Crossing Shelton's mid-afternoon traffic, Foster finally arrived at the house of Clarence Willits, parking his Harley up the street. Willits lived in a small two-bedroom house wedged in between two much larger dwellings. Its exterior appeared intact, if a little shabby, as did the lawn and remnants of a front garden. With a slight breeze blowing against his back, Foster strode up to the front porch, and knocked firmly on the front door. The elder man immediately allowed the towering Foster inside, which immediately heightened the social worker's concern for him. Foster always felt wary about seniors too ready to trust strangers.

Willits led Foster into the front room, where he sat down on a chair across the coffee table from Willits' couch. The interior walls bore a pale green shade. From the northwest corner leaked a brown water stain which spread in width as it trailed down the wall. The rest of the home, the kitchen – which Foster glanced into – and down the hall, appeared intact and tidy. He guessed the neatness resulted more from lack of use, however, than Willits' industriousness as a cleaner.

As they settle in their seats, Foster told the elderly Willits, "I'm a social worker from the county of Cedarwood. My name is Bob Foster, and I'm here to make sure you're okay."

"Well, that's quite nice of you," said Willits, in a shaking voice. "I'm doing okay."

"How's your health?" Foster asked. "Are you feeling well?"

"Oh, yes," he answered, his hand trembling slightly as he rested it upon his chin.

"You look like you're in pretty good shape. How old are you?"

"Eighty-seven," Willits answered.

"What's your date of birth?"

"Uhhh…June 30…1923…"

"What do you attribute to your good health?"

"I eat a lot of yogurt," he said, "and vegetables."

"Do you do your own shopping?"

"Yes, I walk down to the store in downtown Shelton."

"Is that where you get your vegetables?"

"Yes," he said. "You know, I used to work in a vegetable plant for the Clark's company in Sparta."

"Oh, yeah…what did you do?"

"I was foreman for the canning department. We would make sure all the vegetables were packed for the store."

"I see why you might like vegetables so much."

"Yes," he said, shakily reaching for a magazine on the coffee table. "I'm a pretty good cook, too." He held up the magazine in his hand, and said, "I use the recipes from this cuisine magazine."

"That's great," Foster said. "So, you're a chef, huh?"

"Yes…that's what I am, all right."

"Well, the reason I am here is because I received a call from Mrs. Yee from your bank. She was concerned because she thinks you are going to sell your house for much less money than it is worth."

"Yes, I'm going to sell it to my next door neighbor."

"Mrs. Yee says not only are you going to sell the house at a very low price, but you are first going to take out a loan, and then sell the house after putting all the money into it."

"Yes, the roof needs repairing," he said. "You can see the leak in the ceiling. It has to be repaired."

"It seems to me, Mr. Willits, at the price you're going to sell it, the neighbor should be able to afford to pay for the new roof himself."

"Yes, well, he doesn't have much money. He said he'd buy it if I fixed the roof."

"That's real nice of him," Foster said with sarcasm, which escaped Mr. Willits. "What's your neighbor's name?"

Willits' face turned blank, and he stammered quietly as he looked about, as if hoping to find the answer in the furniture surrounding him. "Uhhh…" he mumbled.

Willits fished into his pants pocket for his wallet, from which he poured several business cards onto the coffee table. He picked up the cards, and flipped them slowly, one by one. He peered intently through his frameless glasses at each one, until finally he settled on the sixth card. He placed the remaining cards up closer to his face. After several moments of examination, he showed it to Foster.

"Can you read this?" he asked.

Foster took the card from him, reading aloud, "Ralph Sterling; this is your neighbor?"

"Uhh…uhh…yeah, Sterling…Sterling is his name."

How long have you known Mr. Sterling?"

Willits closed his eyes in brief concentration. "As long as I've lived here," he concluded.

"And how long has that been?"

Willits paused again, trying to remember. Foster shook his head. "It's okay, Mr. Willits. So, how much are you planning to sell this house for?"

"$32, 000," Willits struggled. "$32,000...I think...something like $32,000."

"Mrs. Yee..." Foster paused. "You know, Mrs. Yee at your bank, right?"

"Mrs. Yee...uhh, yes, yes...I know her. She was at my house the other day."

"Right," Foster said. "She thinks your property is worth closer to $480,000, Mr. Willits."

Willits' eyes blinked several times, as he struggled to assimilate this information. "$480,000?" he creaked.

"Yes, that's why she was concerned when she learned you wanted to sell it for $32,000."

Willits mumbled to himself, looked aside from Foster, who studied him carefully.

"Who suggested you should sell your house to Mr. Sterling?"

"Well, he came up to me one day, and said he really likes my house. He asked if I would sell it to him. He told me the house would need a lot of repair, but he would be willing to buy it for $32,000. I wanted to do this for him, because he has helped me so much."

"Oh? What has he done for you?"

"Well, sometimes he shops for me. Other times, he waters my plants...things like that."

"And that's why you want to sell the house to him for $32,000?"

"Yes..." he answered, seemingly oblivious to the bigger picture.

"So, what are you going to do after you sell the house?" Foster asked.

Willits paused again. "What?"

"What are you going to do? Where are you going to live?"

Willits paused even longer. "I don't really know..." he finally said.

"Have you looked for another place to live? Like an apartment, or a board and care facility?"

Willits' eyes brightened, as if he had found something he'd long been looking for. "I called the place in Dalton City…a place I could move to…"

"Do you know what the place was called?"

Willits reached for the stack of business cards once again, which seemed to be his sole connection with the outside world. After thumbing through the stack again, he settled upon a card which belonged to "The Retirement Center of Dalton City."

"The Retirement Center," Foster read aloud. "Is this the place you looked at?"

"Yes," he said. "Well…I didn't actually look at it. I called them once."

"Do you know how much it would cost to live there?"

The vapid gaze returned to Willits' countenance.

"Did they send you any information…a brochure?" Willits looked about him, near the coffee table, as if perhaps the brochure lay nearby, but he had forgotten what he had done with it.

Foster shook his head again as he stared at Mr. Willits. It appeared difficult enough for Willits to respond to each question, let alone to be able to comprehend the enormity of his problem. Like many of the seniors Foster had seen with dementia, Willits seemed able to manage the day to day chores of eating, sleeping, getting dressed, sometimes shopping. Beyond that, organizing and planning for his life proved an extremely difficult task. Foster felt very relieved he had visited the title company, and stopped the sale of Willits' home.

"Do you have any family?" Foster asked, changing the subject.

"My daughter," Willits brightened, as if Foster had finally touched on a subject he felt he could master.

"What's her name?" Foster asked.

"Brenda," Willits answered.

"Where does she live?"

"In Nebrask…no, I mean Oklahoma."

Do you have her address or phone number?"

Willits paused again, and once again reached for the business cards. Foster patiently allowed him to go through his routine, until he came to a well-worn card, which he handed to the social worker. Foster studied the card. "Brenda Sandalow. Is that her name?"

"Yes, it is…" Willits answered. "She got married a few years back…"

Foster jotted down the address and telephone, and dutifully returned the card to the pile on the table. "Does she know about the sale of the house?"

"I think so…" Willits mumbled. "I think I told her…I'm not sure…"

"When was the last time you spoke to her?"

"A week…no a few weeks ago…"

Foster had seen enough. There was no need to continue the interview. Although he did not appear to be in any immediate danger, Mr. Willits certainly could not manage the sale of his home by himself.

"Well, I'm gonna get going, Mr. Willits. Is there any thing in particular you need right now?"

"I can't think of anything>" the elderly man answered.

"Well, then, I'm going to go." Foster left his own business card near the stack. Then he approached Mr. Willits, extending his hand, "Very nice to meet you, sir."

"Nice to meet you as well," Mr. Willits answered. "Thank you for coming by."

Immediately upon returning to the office, Bob Foster met with Ari Davis to refer Clarence Willits for conservatorship investigation. For once, Davis completely agreed with the referral. Foster gave her a copy of the 3701 administered to the Title Company, plus all the information pertaining to the pending sale of the house, Willits' financial situation, and the little information obtained about the daughter.

The following Thursday morning, Patrick Brennan steered his 21-speed road bike around the corner and east to the parking lot adjacent to the Health Complex in Cedarwood. The parking lot –

long the center of controversy regarding the sardine-like fashion in which employee cars are situated – accommodated staff of both the county hospital and the health department offices, the location of Adult Services. Brennan parked his bike in an inner office court-yard near the Big Room, chained securely against a post support-ing the roof overhang.

Brennan traversed four miles each morning and evening from his home in northeast Cedarwood, to the Adult Services office in the southwest. Brennan once calculated his bike had saved he and his family more than $40,000, the estimated amount he would have spent on a car. Although life sometimes becomes hectic on week-ends, when his wife, son, and daughter all tried to get to their si-multaneous activities using one car, he considered his bicycle one of the best investments he'd ever made.

As Brennan glided through the parking lot toward the west em-ployee entrance, he met up with Bob Foster, parking his Harley in its normal space. Foster peeled off his gloves as Brennan sprung off his bike behind him.

"Mornin'" Brennan called, as Foster whirled toward him.

"Oh…morning," Foster said, as he secured his back pack be-hind him. "How's the ride?"

"Oh, only three near-death experiences today," Brennan quipped, as he and the taller Foster entered the building side by side. "I swear, these drivers would as soon run over me as look at me, you know?"

"Geez…" Foster sympathized.

"So how long you had the motorcycle?"

"Oh, about six years," Foster said, "ever since the divorce. I had one before I married, and decided to get one afterward."

"What…you drove a station wagon when you were married?"

"Yeah…believe it or not…even though we only had one kid."

"Donovan, right..?"

"Yeah…"

"How old is he now?"

"Twenty-one," he said. "He's attending a university up north. He comes down to visit every once in a while."

"He has his own car, right?"

Foster glanced quizzically down at Brennan, who continued.

"Well, I just had this comical vision of you taking Donovan to a ball game on your cycle."

"No, no…" Foster chuckled, "we take the car."

"Good, good…" Brennan said. "Boy, those things scare the hell outa me…"

"What, motorcycles?" Foster exclaimed. "As opposed to what you ride everyday…"

Brennan considered his statement for a moment. "Yeah, well…I see what you mean. I guess I feel safer under my own power than a motor?"

"Whatever…" Foster chuckled, his eyebrow raised.

"To each his own, eh…" Brennan said.

"So, isn't there a meeting today?"

"Oh…yeah…" Brennan grumbled. "Oh, well…there goes the morning!"

Sollie Rivers walked into the staff room late Thursday morning, where the rest of the unit had been meeting for ten minutes. His normal, exuberant, boisterous personality had been replaced with a sullen expression and a seething grimace. "Sorry I'm late," he muttered, as he slumped into a straight-backed chair in the far right corner of the room, next to Emma Hayes. From the head of the table, Chuck Corley watched him carefully as the supervisor finished his announcement. Corley then looked up, speaking in his usual soft manner, "I was about to ask if anyone had anything to talk about, Sollie?"

Normally, such an introduction would have brought a sheepish grin to Rivers' face. This morning, he simply glared straight-faced, his jaws clenched. "We've got to do something about the representative payee program!" Rivers growled.

"You saw the note on your desk?" Corley asked.

"Yeah, I saw it…goddammit…excuse my language."

"What happened, Sollie?" Emma nudged him from his right.

"I left a note two weeks ago to write a check for a client named Bennie. Bennie is brain injured, alcoholic, and extremely volatile with poor impulse control. Social security says there's no way he could manage his own money, which is why we are his rep/payee. Well, despite the two weeks notice to Harry, he was still late in notifying accounting to cut the check. Bennie went nuts, called the Board of Supervisors, who of course called Marlene. Now she wants to meet with me to find out why this client is complaining. I don't need this shit, man! It's ridiculous!. And it's all because I can't talk directly with Harry! This is nuts!"

Every social worker or nurse sitting around the table nodded in agreement, or voiced solidarity in their feelings regarding the representative payee program.

"Another time," Rivers continued, "I had been wrestling with Sally Ann for four months trying to set up a rep/payee for Rodney. I filled out all the papers – the agreement, the budget, the doctor's statement, everything – and I turned it into Sally Ann. For two months I waited for the program to pick up the case. Finally, Sally Ann sends back a note telling me to resubmit the application, because she misplaced it. Even though I was pissed, I redid the application, turned it in again, and waiting another month. Then she sent back another note saying she needs me to document whether this man owns any property. Any property...the man's been a disabled alcoholic for most of his life. What damned property is he gonna have?"

"In the meantime, I find out she found the first application under a stack of papers in her office. And it's gonna take another four weeks before the application is turned into Social Security. Meantime, Rodney can't get any money because Social Security won't release any without a rep/payee. It drives me nuts!"

"It's ridiculous, Chuck," Emma Hayes said quietly, sitting next to Rivers, "and it happens all the time. And the other problem is there's no one to talk to about it. Sally Ann is never available, and all she does is send applications back with little post-ems all over them. Harry is never available, now that Sally Ann has told him he doesn't have to talk to us. It's unbelievable how one employee can cut himself off from so many others."

"Yes, I know," Corley nodded. "Patrick, you've had the most experience working with the rep/payee program. Are you still having trouble?"

"No, not recently," Brennan answered from Corley's left. "For a long time I wasn't allowed to talk with him either. I agree with you, Emma: there is no excuse for an employee in the Big Room to be able to simply boycott communication with fellow employees. But anyway, one day I decided I needed an answer to a question in less than the usual week, so I just went up to him and talk to him anyway. For whatever reason, I haven't heard any objection since. I normally use the memo system which – by the way – can take at least a week for an emergency request. But if I need an answer right away, I'll just go up to him!"

"Well, I can't talk to him," Rivers complained. "The last time I tried talking to him, he cussed me out in front of everyone, and told me to get the hell away from his desk. Ever since then, we haven't said anything to each other, and Sally Ann seems to support his position."

"Well, I have to admit it," said Donna Briar, sitting to the left of Brennan. "I don't blame Harry for limiting conversation between himself and other staff. There is no way he can do that job by himself; there are too many cases, and not enough time."

"So, why don't they change it," Rivers snorted. "Either get him some help, or start rejecting cases, or something…"

"Oh, simple…" chimed Bob Foster, sitting across the table from Briar. "It just ain't a priority for the division. Sally Ann has all these conservatorship cases to supervise, in addition to running the rep/payee program. There's just not enough time for both, and the court makes the conservatorships the priority."

"So, why do they continue to even operate the program?" asked Rivers.

"Because Marlene feels it's a commitment the division can't get out of," Foster said.

"It started getting really bad with the drug and alcohol clients," Brennan said.

"What do you mean?" asked Corley.

"You know, a few years ago, when Social Security decided to accept alcoholics and drug addicts as disabled individuals, we received a sudden flood of applications for representative payee. It started taking more than two months for Sally Ann and Harry to process the applications. Social Security would release no money to the client without a representative payee, and suddenly these clients were going a month or more without any money. Well, we know how patient and reasonable these addicts can be: they started calling Harry up, yelling at him: they'd call up and complain to Social Secruity, who would call Harry up and get on his back, too. Harry – who is trained as a clerk, not a social worker – was having to field so many complaints he couldn't get his paper work done. So Sally Ann set up the memo system to protect him from the public. Now the hotline staff handles all the requests from the clients and social security, and communicates them to Harry."

"You know, when I worked in long term case management," said Briar, "we used to handle the rep/payee client decisions ourselves. We'd do all the paper work – including SSI applications – and we would direct accounting in the writing of checks. It worked much better, and took far less time."

"I've offered to help Harry at various times," Brennan added. "I even offered to fill out the applications to be representative payee, and take them down to Social Security myself. But Sally Ann wouldn't go for it. Somehow this program is the last priority for her, but she is not willing to give up any control of it."

Well, it may be coming to a head," Corley said. "This meeting Marlene called you to, Sollie, is going to include myself, Sally Ann, and Harry. Marlene was not happy to learn we were still having problems with the program, two years later."

"Well, I hope so," Rivers said. "For us to have to continually screw around with Harry and Sally Ann about this program is nuts. We're not talking about a whole lot of money here."

On his way in from lunch early Friday afternoon, Patrick Brennan found a note in his message box from a social worker form St. Jerome's Hospital named Amy Medina. The hospital was situated in a huge metropolis to the north of Dalton City. Brennan returned the call right away.

"St. Jerome's Social Services," a female voice answered.

"This is Patrick Brennan, Cedarwood County Adult Protective Services. I got a message you called."

"Yes, thanks for calling," the woman answered. "I got your name from Terrell Matthews, who told me I should call you."

"Why? What's up?" Brennan asked.

"Terrell tells me you're trying to find the whereabouts of his mother, Lucille."

"That's true," Brennan responded. "Do you know where she is?"

"She's right here, on the seventh floor. Her son Calvin dropped her off last night," Medina answered.

"How's she doing?"

"Well, she seems a little weak, and a little cold, and confused as usual. Calvin apparently got tired of her again, and dropped her off."

"You sound like you know Calvin Matthews," Brennan observed.

"Yes, I do," she said emphatically. "In addition to my work in the hospital, I work in a low-cost drop-in clinic down the block. I've seen Calvin quite a bit, because he never works long enough to afford any kind of medical insurance. This isn't the first time he's dropped his mother off like this, either."

"Is Calvin still there?" Brennan asked.

"No, he left last night, said he wouldn't be back until later tonight. I don't know where he went…I'm sure he doesn't have any place to live, which is probably why he couldn't keep Lucille any longer."

"Did he appear drunk?"

"No, Patrick, but he scares me, he always does. Have you ever met him?"

"No, I've never had the pleasure."

"He's short, stocky man, with huge arms. He has a temper too. He could do some real damage if he got real angry."

"Do you know if he's ever harmed his mother?"

"Not directly, but there is no way that woman should be riding around with him, with the places he goes and things he does. He takes her money, spends it, and then just drops her off when he can't handle her anymore. And she won't do a thing to stop him. You need to get her away from him."

"We want to do that, Amy," Brennan said, "but there's the problem with getting her. Is there any way a psychiatrist over there could place Lucille on a hold there, and have her transported to Cedarwood General Hospital?"

"I could check, but I doubt it. This not a real adventurous bunch of doctors here, especially for someone who lives out of the county. Couldn't you come and get her? I'm sure no one here would object to that."

"I'll have to clear this with my supervisor," said Brennan. "Let me talk to him, and I'll call you back."

Brennan hurried into Chuck Corley's office to discuss the latest development. Brennan acknowledged the difficulty – as well as the technical illegality – of implementing a psychiatric hold across county lines. Bob Foster would have a fit. But Brennan reminded Corley that Lucille Matthews is considered a resident of Cedarwood County, and of the corresponding responsibility placed on APS. He also presented the vulnerable position Calvin placed his aged mother in time after time, without apparent concern for her welfare. Brennan said he could place the psychiatric hold based on Lucille's status as a gravely disabled adult: Terrell has said he can no longer provide her food, clothing, and shelter, she can't provide it, and Calvin does not appear to be able to either – even if he did not constantly place his mother at risk. Brennan lobbied that if they did not take this opportunity to get her, they might not have another opportunity any time soon.

"According to Emma, this Calvin is a real sleaze," Brennan said. "He takes her money, spends it on drugs, and then dumps her off- just as he did last night."

"What if the hospital staff at St. Jerome's doesn't cooperate?"

"It sounds like they're pretty interested in avoiding Calvin, if at all possible. It sounds like this Amy Medina will advocate for us over there. I think they'll cooperate."

"This is a pretty unusual move you're making."

"Yeah, I know, but this is an unusual case. We might not have another chance."

"Do they know where Calvin is now?"

"She says he's out, and won't be back until tonight. The time to move is now!"

"Okay," Corley said. "Inform PES about the situation. If they have any questions, they can talk to me. Go get her."

Within two hours, Patrick Brennan stood before the elevator, to take him to the 7th floor at St. Jerome's Hospital. As pre-arranged, Brennan would meet Medina at the nurse's station near Lucille's room. He had called for the ambulance when he reached the hospital, wanting to make the transition as quick as possible; he hoped the paramedics would not take very long.

Brennan entered the elevator with a short, stocky African-American male who appeared to be in his forties. He was dressed rather shabbily in old blue jeans and a short sleeve sweatshirt, which revealed his massive, tattooed biceps. He fit the description Amy Medina had given. The man nodded briefly toward Brennan, dressed much more formally in his pullover sweater and overcoat. As the two men watched the floor lights change, Brennan suddenly held his breath, especially as both men stepped off the elevator on the seventh floor. If this man turned out to be Calvin Matthews – returning to the hospital at this very moment – Brennan's day would very soon become much more complicated.

But then his co-passenger headed in an opposite direction, allowing Brennan to breathe a bit easier. "I'm just paranoid," Brennan mumbled to himself. He turned the corner and stopped at the nurses' station, and informed a tall, light brunette he had come here to see Amy Medina.

"I'm Amy," she said, smiling and holding her hand out to Brennan. "You must be Patrick Brennan."

"I must be," he said, shaking her hand. "Where is Mrs. Matthews?"

"In the room behind you," Medina pointed. "She's been here since last night. She seems to be doing okay physically, except for some congestion in her chest. We're trying to make sure it doesn't become pneumonia. She's quite confused, and she keeps asking for her son."

"Have you seen him?" Brennan asked.

"I haven't seen him at all," she answered. "He dropped her off last night, saying she had a cold or something."

"Can I speak with her?" Brennan asked.

"Sure, go ahead. She's sort of hard of hearing, through, so you'll have to speak up."

Brennan entered the sparse hospital room, where he found an elderly woman, lying in a semi-upright position in the hospital bed. She squinted with her brown eyes as she noticed someone enter the room. "Good mornin'" she called.

"Good morning, Mrs. Matthews," Brennan said. "How are you doing this morning?"

"Okay," she answered in a tired voice. "Are you the doctor?"

"No, I'm a social worker. My name is Patrick Brennan."

"Have you seen my son Calvin?" the woman asked.

"No, ma'am, I haven't," Brennan answered. "Does Calvin take care of you?"

"Yes, sir," she said.

"What's Calvin do for you?"

"Well, he helps me…pay for things…like the rent…"

"Where's he payin' rent now? Does he have an apartment?"

"Yes, sir…"

"Where's the apartment? What city is it in?"

The old woman hesitated as she tried to recall. "It's in Dalton City…no, Plymouth."

"Isn't it Terrell who lives in Plymouth?

"Terrell…oh yeah…."

"So, where is Calvin's apartment…?

"Oh, well..I don't really remember…

"Do you live there with Calvin?"

"Yes, I do…" she mumbled.

"How much rent do you pay?"

"I don't know…Calvin pays the rent."

"Did you go to the apartment last night?"

"I don't remember…I think we just drove around last night."

"How does Calvin pay his share of the rent, Mrs. Matthews?" Brennan asked. "Does he work?"

"No, he pays the rent with my social security, until he can get on his feet."

"How much social security do you get?"

"Uh…I'm not sure…Calvin handles it…about \$300.00 a month."

"I see," Brennan said, the picture getting clearer. This woman seemed to be completely dependent on – and vulnerable to – her son."

"Why are you in the hospital, Mrs. Matthews?"

"Calvin thought I should go to the hospital," she replied. "He said they would take care of me there?"

"What day did you come to the hospital?"

"Um…two, no three days ago..?"

"Do you know what date it was, or which day of the week?"

"No, sir…"

"Do you know today's date?"

She hesitated again, and said, "No, sir, I've been here, but I don't know how long."

"It's okay, Mrs. Matthews, don't worry about it."

Having learned what he needed to know, Brennan spent a few more moment talking with her, and about how she was feeling.

"So, what do you think you'll do once you get out of the hospital?" he asked.

"I don't know."

"Are you tired of moving around all the time?"

"Yes, sir, I surely am!"

"What if I told you I could find you a permanent place to live, where they would fix your meals. There would be someone there to help you."

"That sure would be nice," she said, laying back again the bed. "I just wanna stay in one place. I sure wish Calvin could stay in one place."

"Well, I might be able to arrange for you to go to a place like that," Brennan said.

"That would be nice, sir," she said. She hesitated for a moment, and then asked, "Could Calvin live there, too?"

"I don't think so."

"Well, then I don't know," she said.

"Well, I'll talk to you later, Mrs. Matthews."

Brennan returned to the nurses' station. "The ambulance should be here any time," he said to Medina, who waited there for him. "I'm going to fill out the form for the hold. There is no way she can take care of herself, no can either son. She thinks Calvin is paying the rent somewhere, but I know that isn't true."

Medina looked quickly beyond Brennan and down the hall, and then let out a quiet gasp. "Oh, my God...there he is!"

Brennan turned his head slightly, and looked out the corner of his eye. Walking up the hall was the man in the elevator, quickly approaching Mrs. Matthew's room.

"Is that Calvin?" Brennan asked quickly.

"Yes," she said.

"I knew it! Bloody hell! Could you call security...quickly...? I'd like to have them standing by before I tell Calvin the bad news."

"Good idea!" Medina said, reaching for the phone. "I know how Calvin can be."

As Brennan watched Calvin shuffle into his mother's room, he cursed, "Where the hell's that ambulance? Amy, do you think Calvin will want to take his mother out?"

"I don't think he has anywhere to take her," she said.

"You're probably right," he chattered. "Where the bloody hell's that ambulance?"

Brennan drummed his nervous fingers on the counter, as he finished writing up the psychiatric hold form. Finally, three men in gray suits and black ties sauntered up to the station. The tallest one – whose name tag read "David Lymon" – spoke on a cell phone as he approached. Amy Medina introduced Lymon to Brennan, who quickly explained the situation. Lymon said he had met Calvin Matthews before, and understood his reputation. He spoke quickly to his fellow officers, and then told Brennan in a deep, reassuring voice, "We'll stand by."

Just then, Amy Medina's phone beeped. "There are paramedics downstairs," she told Brennan.

"Good," he said, "we'll wait until we get here."

When the paramedics arrived, Brennan directed them to wait down the hall until he called for them. With the security team behind him, Brennan approached Calvin Matthews.

"Mr. Matthews," he called, pointing to the badge on his sweater. "My name is Patrick Brennan. I'm a social worker from Cedarwood County. Could I speak with you for a moment outside the room?"

Matthews said something briefly to his mother, and then followed Brennan into the hall. Matthews eyed the men in the gray suits, and then asked sharply, "What's goin' on?"

"Mr. Matthews, I'm here to take your mother back to Cedarwood County, to find her a safe and permanent place to live. She can't stay in the hospital, and it isn't safe for her to be without a home."

"What do you mean?" Matthews said sternly. "I'm finding her a place to live. I called a minister of a church, who is looking for a place for us?"

"Do you have a name or a number for this minister?' Brennan asked.

Matthews groped about his clothing with his hands, saying, "I had it somewhere. I must've left it."

"Well, what are you going to do with your mother until you find a place?"

"I'll bring her back to my brother's home until…"

"I spoke to you brother. He can't take her back. He told me what happened last night, and he doesn't think it's safe for anyone to have her, most of all there."

"Well, you can't just take her…"

"Actually, I can, Mr. Matthews. I am authorized to take your mother to Cedarwood County Hospital, since she's gravely disabled, and she has no place to live. It's not safe for her to be on the street."

Matthews started fuming, stepping forward toward Brennan. "Well, I ain't gonna let you take her, goddammit!" Brennan could smell the alcohol already on Matthew's breath.

David Lymon stepped in between them, his two officers behind him. "Mr. Matthews, just calm down now…"

"I ain't gonna calm down. Don't tell me to calm down. He can't take my mother like that."

"I'm afraid he can," said Lymon. "Now, if you can't simmer down, I'm going have to ask you to leave the hospital."

"Shit!" said Matthews. "When am I gonna get ta visit her?"

"Once she gets situated," Brennan told him. "Call that number on my card on Monday, and we can let you know where she is."

Matthews snatched the card from Brennan's hand. "What a bunch of shit!" he shouted. "I'm getting' me a lawyer, man! I'm gonna sue yore asses!"

"Come on, Mr. Matthews," Lymon urged, leading him away from the nurses' station. "There's nothing you can do now. You can talk with them later, and see about your mother." The other security officers surrounded Matthews, leading him away to the elevator. Matthews shouted and cursed every step of the way.

Brennan, in the meantime, motioned to the paramedics. They gently lifted the frail Lucille Matthews onto the gurney. Brennan told her she would be taken to another hospital, where they would take care of her, and find her a nice place to live.

As the gurney rolled toward the elevator, Brennan followed it. Amy Medina waved to him as he left. "Thank you very much." She said. "You have a tough job."

"Thanks," he replied, "it gets interesting sometimes."

By the time Brennan made it back to the office, Cedarwood County Hospital was in an uproar. Apparently, Calvin Matthews issued a series of threats toward St. Jerome's security team as they escorted him out the door. Security Chief David Lymon called Cedarwood County Hospital security, dutifully reporting Calvin had threatened to find a gun, come to the hospital, and free his mother. Frantic messages from the Emergency Room – where Lucille Matthews had been transported for medical clearance – covered Brennan's desk. The ER staff had called in a panic, wanting to know what miscreant would allow a man to come to the hospital brandishing a gun. Brennan assured them he knew nothing about a gun. He informed them of the situation, told them a temporary conservatorship would be sought, which would remain in place until a permanent petition could be completed. An investigation would be conducted. Lucille would be removed from the hospital as soon as possible.

The Cedarwood County hospital security staff remained on alert throughout the weekend. Brennan briefed the on-call social worker for Adult Services on the situation, and how to respond to Calvin should he call: He would be allowed to see his mother next week; Lucille remained on a hold in a secured area of the hospital, and the conservatorship investigator would talk with Calvin next week.

As it turned out, Calvin never appeared at the hospital, and never attempted to contact anyone connected with the county over the weekend. Within a few days, he would come to Lucille's room, ranting and raving as he had at St. Jerome's. At one point, the Dalton City Police Department discovered an outstanding warrant for him, and he was arrested during a subsequent visit to the hospital. But he never became violent, nor did he make specific threats. It seemed as if, on some level, he understood this was the best thing for his mother – even if it meant curtailing his only source of income.

"Cedarwood Adult Services," Donna Briar answered the hotline on the following Wednesday morning. "Can I help you?"

"Good afternoon. I need to make a report of sexual abuse," a female voice stated on the other end of the line.

"Concerning an elderly or disabled client?" Briar clarified.

"A developmentally disabled client," the woman continued.

"Okay," Briar said, "and what is your name?"

"My name is Carla Reinhart," she said. "I'm a special education instructor at American High School in Richland."

"Is this concerning a student of yours?"

"Yes, her name is Nancy Ogden."

"Her address..?"

"1387 Lincoln Circle, Richland."

"The phone number..?"

"555-4678"

"What is Nancy's date of birth?"

"8-14-77...she's nineteen."

"Who lives with her at her address?"

"Her mother, Margaret Ogden, who is about forty..."

"Anyone else..?"

"Her step-father...well, actually, it's Margaret's boyfriend, a man named Bruce Lucas. Also, Nancy's younger sister, Linda, lives there. Linda is nine."

"What is Nancy's diagnosis?"

"She is mildly to moderately developmentally disabled, with an IQ in the upper sixties. She's a little overweight, but with a beautiful smile and long, brown hair."

"Does she have a case worker through the Regional Center?"

"Yes, her name is Joan Parker. She's been her worker for about eight years now."

"Does Nancy work?"

"No, she's attending some vocational rehabilitation classes through school. She's learning various survival skills through the classes, but I doubt she will ever be able to make enough money to support herself."

"Does Nancy have any source of income?"

Yes, she receives supplemental security income, about $650 a month.

"Does she manage it herself?"

"It comes to her mother, who is her representative payee."

"Does she have any physical or medical problems?

"Not really."

"So what happened?"

After school today, Nancy came to visit me in my office, as she does every Wednesday. She is DD, but she is very much nineteen physically. On Wednesday I act as her guidance counselor for her classes. We go over her school work, talk about her classes, other things that might be concerning hr. Anyway, this afternoon she told me her mother's boyfriend – Bruce – has been sexually harassing her."

"What has he been doing?"

"She said he's been hiding in the closet of her bedroom, watching her undress. He has also been saying suggestive things to her, making comments about her figure. Last night, after she found him in the closet, as he was passing by her, her reached out and fondled her breast with his hand."

"How long has this been going on?"

"Well, this is the second time she caught him in the closet. The other time was a few weeks ago. He made some excuse then, but she was still suspicious. But now she is sure. Bruce works at night, but Margaret works during the day. He is usually alone with her after school because Linda goes to soccer practice. Margaret gets home at around six pm.

"Has she told her mother?"

"She's been afraid to. She doesn't think she'd believe her. She says she's also concerned about her sister, because she is becoming older too."

"Where is Nancy now?"

"She's heading home. She takes the bus after she meets with me."

"So she felt safe about returning home?"

"Well, not really…but we didn't know what alternative there was."

"We could send a police officer out to the house to talk to everyone tonight. We'd have to cross report this referral to the police anyway."

"I don't know," Reinhart said, "the police?"

"Did Nancy know you are going to report this to us?" Briar asked.

"Yes, I told her, but I didn't say anything about the police."

"Well, I think if Nancy is going to feel in any way threatened going home, we should send an officer out."

Reinhart paused for a moment. "Actually, that might be a good idea. It would be good for the police to set some boundaries in that home, and let Bruce know people are watching what he's doing. What do you think the police will do?"

"Well, in the case of child abuse, the police usually insist the alleged perpetrator leave the home until an investigation can be completed. If the mother is not willing to kick Bruce out, they might call us and ask to house her somewhere. Do you think Joan Parker would be able to find her a place to stay tonight, if needed?"

"I could call her and ask," Reinhart said. "I've known her for quite a while."

"Good," said Briar. "You call Parker, and I'll call the police and ask for the officer to go out to the home this evening. We will open an investigation on this matter, but exactly when somebody goes out depends on what the police do tonight."

"OK." Reinhart said. "Will you let me know what happens?"

"As soon as I can," Briar told her.

Donna Briar hung up the phone, and immediately dialed the dispatch line for the Richland Police Department. She spoke to a dispatcher named Helen, to whom she explained the situation. The dispatcher said she would send two officers out to the Ogden residence, a little bit after the time Nancy would likely arrive from school. One of the officers would be Kelly Longstreet, who was specially trained and experienced in the assessment of sexual abuse cases.

When a sexual abuse case involved an individual under the age of eighteen, the police will enter the house and determine if the child is safe to remain in the home. If the mother supports the child and her allegations, and insists the alleged abuser leaves, the police will likely let the child remain in the home. But if it appears the mother cannot protect the child, the police will remove the child from the home, and place it in protective custody with Children's Services, who will find some form of shelter home for the child.

With a nineteen year old, however, the situation in different; with a developmentally disabled adult child, the situation can become extremely complicated. Because she is not a minor, even a developmentally disabled adult – unless she has been assigned a conservator by the court – has a right to decide matters of her own health safety. It is thought if she is competent enough to not need a conservator, then she is capable of making these decisions. In Nancy Ogden's case, even though her mother is her representative payee and pays Nancy's bills, Nancy still has a right to decide whether she feels safe in her mother's home, and whether she wants to continue to live there. The role of the Regional Center – which is a case management service for those with developmental disabilities – is to work with and advocate for the client in conjunction with Adult Protective Services, to help the client decide the best, safest option.

Donna Briar quickly entered the referral into the database, knowing there may be addendums once she hears from the police. She alerted the on-call social worker to the possibility of the Richland Police calling for assistance, particularly if Nancy Ogden needs housing for the night.

As it turned out, the on-call social worker received no call overnight, but Briar received one bright and early the next day, from Kelly Longstreet. Longstreet called to report the occurrences at the Ogden residence the night before.

Longstreet said she and her partner arrived at the house at about 5:30 pm. They found Bruce Lucas home, along with Nancy's mother Margaret, as well as Nancy. Linda – Nancy's sister – was at a friend's house. Longstreet took Nancy to a back room to speak with her in private, while the other officer – a tall broad male named O'Neill – kept Margaret and her boyfriend in the front room. Nancy confirmed with Longstreet the report she made to Carla Reinhart: that she found Bruce Lucas hiding in her closet while she was undressing the previous evening; that Lucas had fondled her and made suggestive, lewd remarks to her; that these incidents had occurred more than once. Nancy commented she did not know whether she felt safe there or no, that it would depend on what her mother did.

After Longstreet completed the interview with Nancy, she returned to the front room to confront the mother and the boyfriend. Not surprisingly, the mother became very upset, began screaming at Lucas, demanding that he leave the house. With the additional persuasion of O'Neill and Longstreet, Lucas gathered some clothes and belongings and left, staying he would stay with some friends. Longstreet insisted he give him the name and address at which he could be contacted. The police warned him not to make contact with the Ogden home.

Afterwards, Longstreet talked with Nancy and Margaret Ogden together. She told them a social worker from APS would be involved to work with them further, and warned Margaret it would be her responsibility to protect Nancy, and keep Bruce Lucas away from the house until the investigation could be completed. She told Margaret that a Richland Police detective would be investigating the crime, while APS would be working with them to arrange counseling, and to make certain Nancy's home remained safe and secure.

Longstreet told Briar she felt Margaret seemed determined to protect both her daughters. However, both Longstreet and Briar knew the complexities of sexual abuse cases. The initial shock and rage could fade, and even the belief Margaret currently felt for her daughter could dissipate. To be on the safe side, Longstreet would report the situation to Child Protective Services, for the protection of the nine year old. The officer suggested Adult Protective Services assign a social worker as soon as possible to help protect and advocate for Nancy.

Chuck Corley assigned the case to Emma Hayes, who conducted a home visit to the Ogden house later that day. She reiterated what Officer Longstreet had said the previous night. Both Margaret and Nancy agreed the young woman would remain in the home, and Margaret agreed to call Hayes or the police if Bruce Lucas returned, or if it appeared Margaret would be unable to prevent his return.

Two weeks later at two o'clock pm, Emma Hayes received another phone call from Carla Reinhart. Nancy Ogden had come to her office once more. She said Bruce Lucas had moved back into her house, and her mother began to believe him over the allegations of her daughter. Although Lucas had done nothing else to Nancy, she no longer felt safe living at home, and she no longer felt her mother could protect her. She wanted to live some where else, and she no longer wanted her mother to manage her money.

Hayes immediately called Officer Longstreet and Joan Parker, and they all agreed to meet at the school, before Nancy left. Parker had already arranged for a group home, into which Nancy could move. Hayes brought forms which Nancy could sign to designate Adult Services as her representative payee. Social Security would be notified, and Nancy's SSI checks would eventually be rerouted to Adult Services, where the Representative Payee program would accept the task of paying Nancy's bills for her.

After meeting at the school, Hayes and Longstreet agreed to pay another visit to the Ogden home, to confront Lucas and Margaret. Nancy's whereabouts would remain confidential, until she herself gave consent.

Longstreet informed the gathering that Children's Services had been notified about the situation, and they would see to the safety of Nancy's sister, Linda. The report to CPS would not be revealed to Mrs. Ogden, however, until CPS had a chance to make a determination of the risk to Linda. Longstreet did not want to give Mrs. Ogden and Bruce Lucas a chance to influence what Linda would tell CPS investigators. Longstreet would be notifed by dispatch if Linda ended up in protective custody.

Hayes pulled her car up behind Longstreet's squad car, parking just behind it in front of the Ogden house. Another squad car awaited their arrival down the street and from it emerged the humongous frame of Officer O'Neill. He spoke briefly with Longstreet, and then the trio approached the Ogden's two bedroom rented house, the officers in front as usual. Margaret Ogden and Bruce Lucas greeted the officers and the social worker at the door. Margaret Ogden appeared to be in her forties, grayish-blonde hair, dressed in jeans and a pink, sleeveless blouse. Bruce Lucas appeared younger, thin and wiry, dressed in a T-shirt and blue jeans. He wore his hair combed straight back, and kept a pack of Marlboro's tucked inside his shirt sleeve.

"What do you mean she's left?" Margaret demanded.

"Nancy told us Mr. Lucas had come back to the house," Hayes said, "and she did not feel comfortable living in the house with him there. So she has been provided another place to live until if or when she feels safe returning home."

"And you did this without consulting me?" Ogden complained. "I'm her mother and I have a right…"

"Nancy is nineteen, Mrs. Ogden," Hayes said, "and she is not conserved, meaning she has a right to make decisions for herself."

"But she's retarded," Lucas blurted out.

"But she is still an adult, and she still has a right to make this decision. Now, the investigation into the allegations she made against Mr. Lucas is not completed, but it is clear she does not fell safe living in her house, and she does not feel confident, Mrs. Ogden, that you can sufficiently protect her."

Mrs. Ogden sat down on her sofa. "But how is she going to live. I pay all her bills."

"Nancy has agreed to allow Adult Services to become her representative payee. This means Social Security will be sending her checks to us, and we will see to her food, clothing, and shelter needs."

Ogden and Lucas glanced at each other, a vague expression of panic veiling their faces. "How can you do that? You have no right. We need that…" Mrs. Ogden seemed to catch herself before completing the sentence."

"Nancy had the right, not me," Hayes told her. "Again, she is an adult, and she has the right to exercise that option."

"How do we know you won't just take all her money," Lucas said bitterly.

"How we manage her money is safeguarded by Social Security. And Nancy can rescind the agreement anytime she wants, she knows that."

Mrs. Ogden slumped in resignation of her sofa, but Lucas cursed, "This is a bunch of shit, man!"

O'Neill stood and raised his hands, "Just simmer down, man. Take it easy. We don't want this getting any worse."

"Well, obviously this girl is making things up," Lucas growled, "or maybe this social worker put ideas in her head. I don't know why everyone is taking the word of this retarded kid over me. She never liked me, and she wants to get rid of me."

"She's developmentally delayed, Mr. Lucas," Hayes said, "she's not delusional. Her perception is just as valid as anyone else, she just sometimes has a harder time expressing herself. How long have you been living in this house?"

Lucas answered, "about two and one half years."

"So why would she start making things up now? It doesn't make sense."

"Why did you allow Mr. Lucas to come back here, Mrs. Ogden," Longstreet said. "The last time we spoke, you seemed pretty determined to keep him away."

"Bruce convinced me that he loves me, and that Nancy is making these things up. I don't believe Bruce would do the things she said he did."

"I want you to know, Mrs. Ogden," said Hayes, "what you are experiencing is very common in these cases. It is hard to believe that the man you are in relationship with could sexually abuse your own daughter. But it would still be in your daughter's best interest if he moved out. But now, of course, it's probably too late."

"Shut up!" Lucas snapped. Red with anger, he lunged at Hayes, but O'Neill placed a heavy hand on his shoulder, holding him back. He compelled Lucas to sit in the arm chair across the room.

"I didn't do nothin' man! You're talkin' about me like a freakin' pervert."

"If you don't calm down," O'Neill said, "I'll arrest you right now!"

"Nobody is accusing you of anything," said Hayes. "I'm just telling you how these things often play out."

"Basically, you're making a choice of your boyfriend over your daughter," said Longstreet. "As long as that is your choice, staying away will be Nancy's choice."

Margaret Ogden grew silent, as Lucas fidgeted in his chair. Longstreet and O'Neill stood to leave, when O'Neill received a message on his cell phone.

"O'Neill," he said into the speaker, and then listened for a few moments. "Yeah... okay, I'll let them know."

He turned to Mrs. Ogden, saying, "That was dispatch. Do you know where your daughter is?"

Ogden's eyes grew wide, and she realized she hadn't seen Linda yet.

"She's been taken into protective custody by the police and Children's Services," he said. "An officer and a social worker spoke to her, and she said she also did not feel safe here. She said she had suspected Mr. Lucas for a long time, and she wondered if something like this was happening to her sister."

Longstreet turned to the boyfriend and told him, "I would strongly advise you to move out of here as soon as possible. Your cooperation would be looked upon favorably by investigators, who will be involved in this case for some time. The harder you make it for them, the harder it will be for you."

Longstreet turned toward Margaret again and said, "In any case, I will notify you if your daughter decides to press charges against your boyfriend.

With that, the social worker and the officers left the house.

The following Thursday morning, Chuck Corley addressed the APS staff seated around the conference table. "So, anyway…the all-staff meeting is canceled. I guess the next one will be in two months, unless it is canceled as well."

A quiet grumble of disinterest arose from the unit.

"Now, I understand you have something you wanted to talk about, Emma."

All eyes in the room turned toward Emma Hayes, who sat at Corley's left. Hayes had a quiet yet eloquent and compelling way of speaking. She smiled easily, even if what she had to say seemed less than happy. The crew always enjoyed listening to her, no matter what she had to say.

Hayes smiled and said, "It concerns a case I have. Actually, Patrick, it was one you went out on first."

"Oh?" Brennan said, his dark eyebrow raised above his right eye. "Which one would that be?"

"You know…Mrs. Stokely…the woman who lived in Cedar-wood City, but then her sister died, and she moved in with a friend – Doris Hubbard – in Maple Creek.

"Oh, yeah," he said. "I went out to make certain she's being cared for properly, and not being taken advantage of. So what's the deal?"

"Actually, Patrick, you mentioned in your notes you saw an elderly gentleman in another room of Mrs. Hubbard's".

"Oh, yeah…I remember that," Brennan said. "I'd gone out to check on Stokely. The thought crossed my mind that perhaps he lived there as well, but I decided to stick to the matter at hand."

"Yeah, well…" Hayes said, rolling her eyes toward Brennan, "the thought crossed Chuck's mind as well. In addition to the gentleman you saw, I found another woman living there. Mrs. Hubbard is running an unlicensed board and care, and now I'm going to have to call the state licensing office to make a report."

"Oops", Bob Foster hooted from Corley's right.

"Yeah," Hayes shrugged. "How come you didn't call the licensing board, Patrick?"

"Emma, I was just happy Stokely didn't appear to be in any trouble. She's well cared for, the place is immaculate, Hubbard doesn't seem to be taking advantage or her, and she pays what is certainly an affordable price for her stay. I didn't want to look any deeper into this."

"Yeah, well, neither do I," Hayes said. "Both the man and the woman seem to be in the same situation. They are not likely to find a better situation of care for themselves, and I really don't want to have to report this. Anywhere else they end up is going to be inferior."

"Are you sure you have to report it?" Rhonda Pagan suggested. "I thought you had to have more then six persons residing in a home before it is considered a board and care."

"No," said Hayes, "I did some checking. Apparently if any unrelated person resides in a home, where they are being provided care for at least some of their activities of daily living, the home is considered a residential care home, and it has to be licensed."

"Of course you have to report it," Ari Davis spoke up, shaking her head in disbelief. "You can't leave her in an unlicensed board & care."

"But what options does she have?" Hayes said. "Here, she's happy, she's well taken care of; she is around people she knows and likes. She has her own room. Anywhere else, she will be miserable."

"It's not really an easy question, Ari," Rivers interjected. "There are regulations, and there is the question of liability, should something happen there. But on the other hand, a disaster could happen even if she lived in a licensed board & care. We're supposed to advocate for our client, and it sounds like this is where the client is most happy, and well cared for."

"Oh, Sollie," Davis said. "How can you say that? You know eventually this woman is going to have to move away. Sooner or later it will be discovered she's living in an unlicensed board and care, and she will have to move. You might as well begin to look now as later. Plus, we already know it's an unlicensed board and care. We're required by law to report it. We just can't ignore that."

"I know", Hayes said, "but it's so ridiculous. Our 'intervention' is going to make it, like, a whole lost worse than it is now."

'Yeah," Rivers said, "things are not that clear cut, Ari. There has to be some room for flexibility, particularly when a client's welfare and happiness are at stake."

"I know that, Sollie," Davis exclaimed, "but nothing good is going to come of ignoring the situation."

"Well, it seems really stupid to move her," Rivers said. "Mrs. Stokely knows her circumstances, and she seems quite happy there."

"The same goes for the other two residents," Hayes agreed. "They are going to be far more unhappy somewhere else."

"Emma, you have to…" Davis practically shouted.

"Okay, that's enough," Corley interrupted. "I'm sorry, Emma, but we have to report it. If something should happen in that home – if there was a fire or some other accident in which one of those persons were hurt – and we did not report it as an unlicensed facility, we could be in big trouble."

"I agree," Bob Foster interjected. "It's really too bad there's such a shortage of low-cost board and cares."

"Maybe licensing will give Mrs. Hubbard a chance to gain her license," said Sollie Rivers.

"Yeah, but it's my bet they won't let those people stay there until she gets it," said Foster.

"I'm sorry, Emma. You're going to have to call state licensing.

"Yeah, I guess…" Hayes frumped.

"Whatever…" Rivers shook his head. "Stupid law…"

Emma Hayes remained involved in the Nancy Ogden case while CPS continued with Linda Ogden. Although Children's Services found no sexual abuse had actually been inflicted upon Linda, the girl felt uncomfortable enough to stay away from the house as well. The CPS social worker reminded Margaret that the pattern in these cases often involved sexual abuse of the older sibling, eventually leading to abuse of the younger if not checked.

Succumbing to the pressures of APS and CPS, as well as pleas from her younger daughter, Margaret Ogden finally forced Bruce Lucas out of her home. She summoned Officer Longstreet to the home, and Longstreet and O'Neill escorted the livid Lucas out of the home. With the help of Emma Hayes, Mrs. Ogden filed a restraining order against Lucas, which forbade him to approach within 1000 yards of the residence. She also filed formal charges against him. Once Ogden forced Lucas out of the home, CPS returned Linda to her mother, since no abuse had actually fallen upon her.

Eventually, Hayes facilitated a meeting between Nancy and her tearful mother, who began to see beyond the denial of the incident. The mother and daughter used the time to clear some of the air, and both agreed to attend counseling together. Hayes felt certain Mrs. Ogden's own childhood and adolescence involved a history of some kind of abuse; sexual abuse can be a pervasive, intergenerational blight.

It would be some time before Nancy and Mrs. Ogden would be totally reconciled – if ever. In the meantime, Nancy decided to remain out of her mother's home, to continue with her adult life, as it should be. Eventually she moved out of the group home and, with a roommate she met through the Regional Center, moved into her own apartment. She also entered into individual counseling, to help her gain some perspective and closure on the incidents involving Bruce Lucas.

Sexual abuse can be difficult, Hayes often told her, but she did not have to let it ruin her life.

Sollie Rivers slumped into a chair in the Bullpen, while Donna Briar finished taking another referral. Rivers watched Bob Foster write down some notes, while he heard Briar end her conversation. "Okay...we'll take it," she said. "Someone will be out to see her next week...okay...bye-bye."

Briar hung up the phone and moaned, "Oh, God...another one of these..."

"What's that, Donna?" Rivers asked.

"Another 'feces and urine' referral," Briar reported.

"Uugghhh!" Foster groaned, feigning a shiver.

"Yeah...a neighbor says there's feces and urine every-where...she's never changed...she never makes it to the bathroom on time...nobody's taking care of her..."

"And how long has this been going on?" Foster asked suspiciously.

"Oh, months..." Briar said. "Forever..."

"What...does this neighbor take regular readings on the feces monitor or something?" Foster asked.

"I guess..."

"You know, it all comes down to poop," Rivers declared.

Patrick Brennan turned his head from his laptop, while Donna Briar raised her eyes about the case file she studied.

"What?" Briar asked.

"It all comes down to poop," he repeated. "We have this fixation with poop. As soon as a referent says the person is pooping in her bed, or pooping in her pants, we go running out there. They even want us to take them to the hospital when there's poop...like that's going to help, somehow."

"Oh, yeah...I know," said Foster. "I love these. You expect to walk into a house knee deep in crap, with pee dripping from the walls, then you find out the old woman had one accident seven months ago."

"Yeah...," agreed Rivers.

"Or the other one's I like," said Foster, "...is when they report their neighbor has no food. You ask 'em how long this has been goin' on, and the say "'for weeks'.

"Well, bloody hell!" Brennan said, holding his hand to his ear, mocking the phone conversation. "Then, I guess they must be dead, right? It's amazing what people don't think about…"

"The question is," Rivers said. "How much poop is too much?"

"What do you mean?" Foster queried.

"How much poop makes a person holdable? If they poop in their pants once; twice; is there a certain depth of poop we need to look at?"

"Good questions," Rivers said. "Sounds like a topic worth exploring. Maybe we need a committee."

"Well, we definitely need a policy statement on this," Brennan concluded.

"We'll get right on it."

"Absolutely…"

"Good thing I got my master's degree, so I can understand these complicated issues."

Chapter 6
JUNE

Over the upcoming weeks, Ari Davis filed a petition with Superior Court for appointment of the Public Guardian as permanent conservator for Lucille Matthews – a petition readily granted. Calvin Matthews would be restricted to supervised visits, with no access whatsoever to her money. The Public Guardian granted Terrell and Maggie unsupervised visitation, while the assigned Deputy Public Guardian placed Mrs. Matthews in a residential care facility, where she continually received the care and supervision she needed.

At the same time, Davis filed for Temporary Conservatorship over Clarence Willits – which essentially grants the Public Guardian authority over Willits' person and estate – until the matter of permanent conservatorship could be more thoroughly investigated. The focal point of the investigation would be to determine if Willits' daughter would be suitable as a conservator and, then, to arrange the transfer of Willits' case to Oklahoma. The Temporary Conservatorship, or T-Con, would protect Willits' estate until the house sale could be resolved, and the permanent conservatorship could be established.

Apparently the Sterlings – Willits' fraudulent next door neighbors – had a friend who worked at the county's newspaper called The Cedarwood Times. For within a week, a blistering article appeared in the Times, in which the neighbors criticized the county's "strong arm tactics" in preventing an old man from doing what he wished with his property. The article compared the county's intervention to that of a "fascist state", and put forth the well-worn conservative argument that the government is far too involved in the affairs of private citizens.

Ari Davis clipped the article out of the Times, and hung it up on her baffle for the office to see. "These damned newspapers," she cried. "If we hadn't protected his house, they would have blamed us for not protecting his house."

Foster and Corley, in conference, minimized the article. Once again, Foster complained, the media made judgments based on very little information, and without a full understanding of the circumstances, or the long-term consequences of Mr. Willet's decision.

After the unit meeting the following Thursday, Sandra entered the Bullpen, a Cheshire cat grin highlighting her face. "Who's on?" she chortled.

Bob Foster whirled slowly in his seat, raised his eyebrows, and carefully asked, "Why do you want to know?"

"I thought it might be you," Sandra giggled. "You've got a visitor."

"Who is it?"

"Gladys," Sandra giggled. "It's your lucky day, Bobby."

"Uugghh…" Foster moaned, rubbing his fingers over his eyebrows.

Rhonda Pagan, gathering forms from the document shelf, asked, "Who is this Gladys I keep hearing about? I've never met her."

"You've never met her?" Foster perked up. "Rhonda, this would be a perfect opportunity…"

"Ummm," Pagan paused. "No, thanks…I'm curious, but not that curious!"

"Well," Briar said, noticing the commotion. "Gladys is sort of the mascot of the division. Several years ago she was featured in a film this division made about the aging process. Ever since then, she's been Marlene's little pet…"

"That's her," Sandra laughed, "and it's Bob Foster's turn."

"Well, what does she want today?" Foster asked.

"Oh, the usual…she's complaining that her check was never mailed, when we know it was. She probably wants to bitch about something else, too. One of her 'friends' brought her here."

"Uugghh…" Foster moaned again.

"So, is Gladys a rep/payee client?" Pagan asked.

"Yes, finally," Briar explained. "They tried to conserve her once, but she beat it. We tried placing her in a board and care, but she wouldn't stay. We finally got her to agree to let us be her rep/payee, because she kept getting kicked out of apartments and hotel rooms."

"Why does she get kicked out?" Pagan asked.

"Well, in addition to not paying the rent," Briar said, "the usual things: partying, drinking, thrashing the rooms, having men over all hours of the night. She used to do all these things on the street corners and bars. Now she's doing them in hotel rooms, but just not as much. Maybe she's just getting tired," Foster said.

"How old is this woman?" Pagan asked.

"What, Bob, about eighty-nine..." Briar asked.

"Eighty-nine, ninety-five, a hundred and twelve...what the hell difference does it make? She's gonna outlive me, I'll tell you that."

"Eighty-nine," Pagan gasped, "with men over all hours of the night?"

"Yeah," Foster continued, "in exchange for portions of her SSA check, they give her favors: rides to places, alcohol, God knows what else..."

"Wow...," Pagan said.

"Have you ever seen her?" Briar asked.

"Not that I know of," Pagan answered.

"Well, then..." Foster said, leading the nurse by the hand. "You're in for a treat. You go watch from the reception area, for an introduction to our little Gladys...

Rhonda Pagan took a seat at a desk behind Sandra to watch the proceedings. Bob Foster opened the door to the lobby, and called out, "Gladys."

From a cushioned seat across the small lobby, an old woman arose from her seat, where a younger, dark-haired gentleman sat beside her. When she made it completely to her feet, Gladys stood perhaps four foot, eight inches, but her back hunched severely, bringing her stature down to about four foot four. She wore a purple down windbreaker over a gray house dress, she steadied her frame with a thin, wrinkled hand clutching a four-pronged, aluminum cane. Age and wrinkles had altered her face, so she wore a perpetual smile which served as both a grin and a grimace. One could picture her in front of the gingerbread house, luring poor

Hansel and Gretel to their demise. Whether she spoke or screamed or laughed, she always seemed to do it with a cackle.

From the desk, Pagan watched fascinated as the woman slowly but unrelentingly hobbled toward the looming Bob Foster. Gladys stopped at the social worker's feet, and craned her neck skyward to look him straight in the eye. "It's about goddamn time," she said. "What the hell took you so long? Think I have nothin' to do but wait here in the goddamn…"

"Oh, my God," Pagan gasped, as she grinned and shook her head.

"Yep," Sandra called, over her shoulder.

Bob Foster followed Gladys into the interview room, and watched her struggle to her seat. As soon as the social worker sat down, the old woman stared him in the eye and squawked, "I've talked to you before."

"That's right, Gladys," Foster said. "What can I do for you to-day?"

"I'll tell you what you can do for me…," she snipped, "you can make sure my goddamn checks get to me, that's what you can do!"

"Well, according to the computer, your check went out last Thursday, like it does every week. What you need to do is go back to you room and wait for your mail."

"I want my check right now!" she demanded.

"It's already been mailed, Gladys," Foster said. "Your check is in the mail. I can't give you a check today."

"Well, what the hell did I come here for, then?" Gladys screeched.

"Beats the hell out of me, Gladys," Forster stared back at her. "You come here every week. You don't have to come here."

"Well, why isn't my whole check just mailed to me? " Gladys said. "Why do I get it in these little drips and drabs?"

"You remember," Foster explained with the patience of Job, "Social Security won't pay you unless you have a rep-payee …otherwise you spend it on booze and other stuff."

"That's a damned lie," she shouted. "I don't drink."

"Well, Social Security ain't gonna give you your checks," Foster growled back. "So you can take it up with them."

"Well, god-damn it, they can't do this to me," she slapped her frail hand upon the table. "I oughta knock you up side your head…"

"Yeah, well you still ain't getting a check," Foster assured her. "So what else can I do for you?"

The two combatants stared resolutely at each other, battle-hardened veterans an eternal public assistance conflict."

"Well…can I get a bus pass?"

"What do you need a bus pass for, Gladys? You've got a ride sitting in the lobby."

"What…oh, yeah…yeah," she said, fishing inside her purse. Foster rolled his eyes.

"Well, can I get a food voucher?"

"You just have to come away with something, don't you, Gladys?" Foster barked, grinning. "Sure, I'll get you a food voucher…but it'll be charged against your account."

"Fine, honey…," Gladys squealed, suddenly all sweetness and light. "Thank you, darlin'."

"Fine, Gladys. Why don't you wait out in the lobby, and I'll get you your voucher."

"Okay…what's your name again?"

"Bob."

"Oh, yeah…Bob," Gladys beamed sweetly. "Thank you, Bob."

Gladys shuffled back out the door and to her seat, where she waited until Foster fetched the food voucher for the grocery store. After Foster ushered her out the front door, and saw her to the parking lot, he found Rhonda Pagan at the inside door, grinning from ear to ear.

"Aren't you nice?" she kidded. "You gave that sweet old lady a voucher."

"Yeah…I probably shouldn't, 'cause she'll just go out and trade it for booze. But at least it kept her from yelling".

"You're a great humanitarian, Bob."

One of the most interesting and enigmatic clients of APS was a gnome-like denizen of Cedarwood County named Kevin Devany. The referral to Adult Services came from Devany's landlady, Mrs. LaVena Owens. She reported Devany – at fifty-eight years of age – remained dependent on his mother for emotional and financial support. Devany's mother dad recently died, leaving Devany on his own. Owens felt concerned that Devany would not be able to care for himself. In addition, within a month, she would be forced to evict him from his premises.

Sollie Rivers found Kevin Devany on a warm June Monday afternoon, in an upstairs studio apartment in Corning, for which Devany's mother had paid for eighteen years. The apartment was attached to a larger home which Owens both lived in and owned. Owens had kept Devany all these years in deference to his mother, with whom Owens had been close friends. But when the mother died, Owens decided she could no longer allow Devany to reside there – and for good reason.

One problem, said the landlord, was Devany would not be able to pay his bills, since his mother did it for him. She also apparently shopped for him, bringing him food which he would somehow prepare for himself – normally on a hot plate inside his studio apartment. Devany had once worked for the Internal Revenue Service as an auditor, a career from which he earned a substantial living. But at age forty-eight, he apparently suffered some kind of breakdown, during which he lost his life savings, and landed in the hospital for several weeks. The details of the incident remained unclear as neither Devany nor his mother ever revealed them. But ever since then, he relied almost totally on his mother for sustenance, something the woman apparently agreed to provide. Devany rarely left the apartment, and when he did it was usually to purchase alcohol. Otherwise, he would sit at home, watch TV, eat, and drink. This ritual apparently comprised the extent of his existence.

Devany's other problem, Owens reported, was his hygiene. He reportedly never washed, his clothes were never laundered; his hair remained dirty and unkempt. His apartment was said to have accumulated a corresponding odor, which had spread to the point of offending the neighbors. Despite numerous warnings, Devany seemed unable to defuse the smell. Since it seemed unlikely he would change, Owens said, he would have to move.

Rivers – who seemed to specialize in the oddest characters in the county – found Devany in his upstairs apartment. The door to Devany's apartment stood slightly ajar, so Rivers – his pony tail waving behind him – bounded up the stairs. He pushed the door open slightly, and called in, "Mr. Devany?" He found Devany seated in a grimy gray upholstered arm chair, on a bare, worn wooden floor. He stared intently at the 24-inch color television no more than seven feet away from him. In the left corner of the one room apartment slumped a worn and weathered, sheet-less mattress, upon which Devany slept. A small side table rested beside the arm chair. In the right hand corner on a metal card table perched a hot plate and a toaster over, next to which stood a metal folding chair. Next to the card table stood a small refrigerator unit. No other furnishings or decorations dressed the apartment; a dingy, pealing white paint covered the walls; levered blinds darkened the windows.

When Rivers entered the apartment, his knees nearly buckled from the power of the pungency. The odor emanated from Devany – Rivers soon determined the appropriate distance at which to stand from him – but seemed to have permeated the walls and floor.

His tangled mop of long gray hair spread about his head and face; his beard seemed an unending nest covering his face and his skull, dangling some eighteen inches from his chin. The tip of his beard narrowed to a point, the accumulated grease and saliva sculpting the follicles to a barbed tip. Devany's skin bore a pasty, grayish shade, partially from his lifestyle, and partially from the compounding layers of dirt. He wore a stained gray long-sleeve cotton shirt, and a pair of blue jean coveralls which appeared equally worn. He seemed quite content while watching his television, remote firmly in his hand. But as soon as he saw the social worker, he physically twitched, and a wild look of fright transformed his face and eyes. The remote began to quake in his hands.

"I didn't mean to startle you," Rivers called. "I'm Sollie Rivers, a social worker for the county. I received a report that you are going to have to move out of the apartment, so I am here to see if I can help you in any way.

"Oh, Mr. Rivers," called Devany, in a quivering, almost childlike, slightly British accent. "I'm so scared. What am I going to do? My mother has died, Mr. Rivers, and I have no one in the world. I have no money, and I don't know where I'm going to." His lower lip began to quiver.

Rivers studied Devany for a moment, determining the best approach to use with him. Rivers grabbed the metal folding chair and dragged it a few feet beside the arm chair, but still a breathable distance away.

"It's okay, Mr. Devany," Rivers said. "I'm going to help you. How are you doing now?"

"I'm afraid, Mr. Rivers, I'm scared," Devany's lower lip curled out, as if he neared weeping.

"I know. But let me find out a little about you."

Devany told Rivers he believed he had no major medical problem, but he had not actually seen a doctor in quite a while. He did not know for certain if he had medical insurance. He had no income, as his mother paid for everything, even shopped for him. Devany did not know whether his mother had left him any money, but thought perhaps the landlord would know. Rivers made a mental note to visit Mrs. Owens when he left Devany.

"Do you have food right now?" asked Rivers.

"A little," answered Devany. "Oh, I'm so scared…"

"Let me look in your refrigerator," Rivers said, already inching toward the kitchen area. Inside the fridge he found a carton of old Chinese food, some ketchup, a jug bottle of wine, and a bowl of some unidentified substance that sat in the back corner.

Rivers stepped over to the bathroom to take a quick look. The smell which came from Devany intensified in the bathroom. Although the plumbing seemed to work, long-standing stains from various sources covered the toilet and the sink. On the other hand, newspapers, boxes, tools, shredded clothing and other items filled the bone-dry bathtub. It obviously had not been appropriately used for many years.

"Don't you ever take a bath?" Rivers asked.

A look of horror covered Devany's slovenly face. "Oh, no, Mr. Rivers…"

"Why not…?" Rivers asked.

"I'm afraid," Devany whined, curling his lip downward.

"Afraid of what…?"

Devany hesitated, and then sniveled, "…of water."

"You're kidding!!" Rivers exclaimed, momentarily forgetting himself.

"No, Mr. Rivers, I'm not," Devany lowered his eyes.

"So you don't wash at all?"

Devany curled his lip again, and shook his mop of hair.

"Ever..?""

His head waggled again.

"Whew!" Rivers shuddered. "So, when do you have to move out?" returning to Devany's side.

"At the end of the month, I think," Devany worried. "I have no where to go, and I don't know what to do."

"Well, the first thing we have to do is find out what kind of income you're going to have. Then, we'll look for a place to live."

Rivers found out from Devany he worked for the IRS for twenty two years, before his breakdown in 1978. Devany never applied for Social Security Disability, which means he should be eligible for Social Security at this point."

"First thing we'll do," Rivers told him, "is go down to the Social Security and apply for your income."

Through his discussions with Mrs. Owens – who knew Kevin Devany when he was a child – Sollie Rivers discovered neither he nor his mother realized – or likely cared – when he reached fifty-five years, he could apply for his pension. He could have also applied for Social Security Disability, had he been diagnosed by a physician. Instead, Devany relied on his mother for subsistence. Unfortunately, Devany's mother spent most of her savings on Devany, and died with little to will him.

Rivers arranged – through much coaxing and hand-holding – for a doctor at the county hospital to examine Devany. The physician found Devany to be in good physical shape, except for a case of hypertension, and some cirrhosis of the liver due to his years of excessive drinking. At a subsequent appointment, Rivers arranged for a psychiatric evaluation, which revealed Devany suffered from depression, generalized anxiety disorder, fixed anxiety disorder, and alcoholism.

Try as he might, Rivers could not convince Devany to bathe, or to wash in any way. It never became clear why Devany feared water so, but it was evident he would not wash. The best Rivers could convince him to do is put on new clothes. Whenever Rivers interviewed him in one of the small interview rooms at Adult Services, he would push open the window to the outside, to allow as much fresh air to enter and diffuse as much of the man's boy odor as possible.

That odor, as much as anything else, prevented Rivers from placing Devany in a residential care home. Such a home would almost be perfect for Devany: there would be people to provide his meals, to take care of him, to comfort him during his anxious episodes. But as soon as RCF staff saw him and smelled him, they immediately closed the doors to him. Since Devany would not be allowed to drink, his interest in the RCF's plummeted.

Rivers theorized Devany had always used alcohol as sort of a self-administered tranquilizer. For a good part of his adult life, he could control his consumption of liquor which apparently kept him sedated enough to allow him to function on his job. But that ended with Devany's break – the immediate cause of which Rivers could never determine; a wayward investment; a woman; a stroke. Nothing could be determined because Devany never sought medical help.

Since then, the man's consumption of alcohol continued to grow alongside his fears. Between his drinking and his terror, Kevin Devany became an emotional vegetable, virtually unable to manage his life without help.

Finally, Rivers had to place him at the Wayside Inn. He convinced Devany to allow the county to be his representative payee. He arranged for a monthly payment for the motel room; he ordered meals on wheels on a daily basis; and the seedy, grimy Kevin Devany settled into the seedy, grimy Wayside Inn.

Chapter 7
JULY

On a warm July Friday, Donna Briar and Bob Foster sat in the Bullpen, each working on a referral for Adult Protective Services. Sollie Rivers wandered in to pick out a SEDAA 434 form, which the workers fill out to complete their investigations. As Rivers reached for the document Rhonda Pagan walked quietly up behind him. She nudged him playfully with her shoulder. "Hi, Sollie," she whispered musically.

Rivers turned and smiled as brightly back. "Good morning, Ronnie," he said quietly, checking to see the phone workers busy with their paperwork. "You look beautiful this morning."

"Thanks," Pagan said, hugging his arm and nuzzling his cheek. "Come on, let's go for a walk."

Rivers took her hand, as they walked side by side, eye to eye across the Big Room. When the couple seemed a safe distance away, Briar and Foster peered out from behind their baffles. Foster than turned to his partner with a big grin, and said, "Ronnie?!" What's going on there?"

"They're an item," Briar giggled.

"How long has this been going on?" Foster asked.

"Several weeks," Briar said. "I see them in the courtyard together a few times a day, and I know they leave work together – and arrive in the morning together – on a regular basis. I think it's cute."

"Uhhh…yeah," Foster grunted.

Briar and her big colleague studied the couple for a few more moments, watching them walk hand in hand through the courtyard, giggling and chatting like high school kids at the soda shop.

The phone workers exchanged amused glances again. "Young love…" Foster said.

"Isn't it wonderful?" Briar finished.

On his way to visit a client in Bristol the next morning, Sollie Rivers drove out to the Wayside Inn to visit Mr. Devany. He parked his car on the north end of the horseshoe drive, and walked back to room 43. Through the wide open door of the room, Rivers found a very startling sight: Kevin Devany, perched on a chair on the other side other motel room bed, stark naked as the day of his birth. His skin appeared pale and wrinkled; his hair and beard gray and mussed. His gray shirt and coveralls lay draped over the bed, and he sat rather nonplused, gazing at the television on the other side of the room. Rivers turned his eyes away for a moment, and then looked reluctantly toward the unlovely Devany. The old gnome had not yet noticed the social worker, when Rivers called toward him.

"Hey, Mr.Devany…"

Devany nearly jumped out of what remained of his skin. "Mr. Rivers," he mumbled. He meekly attempted to draw some bed covers around him.

"Mr. Devany…uhh, do you always sit around your motel room naked with door open?"

"Well…not always…," Devany whined. "I was sort of hot in my clothes, so I…"

"Has anyone complained?" Rivers asked.

"Not as far as I know…"

"Well, you better keep the door closed, or somebody will."

"Yes, Mr. Rivers…"

Rivers thought for a moment, and then decided at the Wayside Inn Devany's little peccadillos probably would go totally unnoticed.

"Since you're naked anyway," Rivers said, stepping in and closing the door, but not shut tight, "did you take a bath, by chance?"

"Uhh…no…"

"Well, I thought since you went to all the trouble…"

Rivers chuckled, trying to inject some humor. Devany didn't see it.

Devany reported to Rivers he continued to receive meals on wheels. He also acknowledged receiving his twenty-five dollars a week allowance from the rep/payee program. Devany said he would take it down to the mini-market three blocks away, where he would cash the check. He denied buying liquor with it, but since Devany could see an empty bottle of whiskey in the trash, he knew Devany was lying. But since Devany could not be forced to accept treatment for his drinking, Rivers knew there was nothing he could do about it but try to limit the damage.

Rivers swore the absolute worse drug in the world was alcohol.

Rivers told Devany he would remain in the motel indefinitely. He wondered if Devany would agree to go to a board and care yet, but Devany declined. Rivers said he would check on him in a couple of weeks.

Brenda Sandalow – Clarence Willit's daughter, whom Ari Davis located in Oklahoma – seemed quite appalled when the extent of the situation had been explained to her. She actually knew the Sterling's next door, and she knew that her father had considered selling the house to them. She had no idea, however, that her father would be willing to part with his domain for so little money, and certainly no clue that Sterling would be willing to take advantage of him that way. There was no doubt on the daughter's part that – contrary to the view expressed by the Times – the government had intervened appropriately.

Over the following six weeks, the court granted the Public Guardian conservatorship of estate, and Mr. Willits moved to a residential care home near his daughter in Oklahoma. Eventually, when his home sold for the proper amount, the estate would be turned over to the daughter, who would manage and protect it for her father and his interests.

The next call Sollie Rivers received on Kevin Devany came from the Cedarwood City Police Department three weeks later. They told Rivers they had responded to a call the previous night at The Wayside Inn. Mr. Patel, the proprietor, complained of Mr. Devany and his hygienic habits. The police found Devany in his room very intoxicated, and lying in a pool of his own feces and urine. The police feared he might have had a cardiovascular accident induced by the alcohol. They called an ambulance, and had him transported to county general hospital on a psychiatric hold.

Rivers took the call, even though he had closed the APS case a week prior, while Devany remained on the rep/payee program. Rivers learned from the hospital that Devany, indeed, has suffered a stroke. Some right side paralysis remained, which compromised both his speech and his ambulation. However, he could still convey to the hospital staff "I'm scared", and he still refused to bathe, although he finally succumbed to a sponge bath. After discharge, he would be placed in a residential care home in Brystol, using money he had inherited from the sale of his late mother's house. The representative payee program would have to be notified – as soon as possible, to accommodate the lethargic process – that Devany would be moving.

Since Sollie Rivers closed the case, Patrick Brennan took the next referral concerning Kevin Devany. Brennan talked to Rosie Onato, manager of the Homefires Residential Care Home. She informed Brennan Devany would be issued a thirty day notice, asking him to vacate the premises. She reported he had become threatening and violent toward the staff, obstinately refusing to bathe. His odor had grown intolerable. He apparently would often sit in a chair, soiled in his own feces, refusing to move. He'd swing at attendants if they tried to move him, and become hostile if they tried to clean him up. He grew more paranoid and anxious by the day, Onato told the social worker, but he continued to ambulate – when he chose to – with a walker.

Brennan consulted with the residential care ombudsman office. The State Department of Licensing contracted with the ombudsman office, to act as a watchdog over residential care homes and skilled nursing facilities in the county. Any potential violation of rights and services accorded residents in these facilities were duly investigated by the ombudsman.

Barbara Bently of the ombudsman office agreed that Homefires could legally ask Mr. Devany to leave. She had already investigated the situation, and indeed it appeared that Devany needed a higher level of care, and supervision that Homefires could not provide. Brennan suggested the only other facility that might be appropriate was the county's secured gero-psychiatric facility, which specialized in the treatment of psychiatric facilities afflicting the elderly. The gero-psych unit was a special wing of Cedarwood County General Hospital. Confinement there would likely require a mental health conservatorship.

Patrick Brennan arrived at the Homefires Residential Care Home on a hot July Tuesday afternoon, to pick up Mr. Devany. When he arrived at the facility, Brennan dialed PES to arrange for the ambulance. The triage nurse told him it would be at least ninety minutes before an ambulance could respond to the site. Since the facility was within five miles of Cedarwood General Hospital, Brennan told the nurse he would bring Devany in himself.

Borrowing a couple of large size plastic trash bags from the facility, Brennan completely covered the back seat of the Taurus. He then rolled down every window in the car. Although it appeared Devany had not yet soiled himself that day, Brennan felt the rest of the APS staff – particularly those who might have to use the car someday – would appreciate his diligence.

Devany seemed to respond neutrally to Brennan, who identified himself as a colleague of Sollie Rivers – which seemed to ease the situation. Although Devany mildly resisted at first, he finally gathered the personal items he stored in a trash bag. Brennan placed the belongings in the trunk, and Devany ambled out to the car behind him. Once again – as Brennan had often noted - these clients seem to know on some level when it is time to go.

Within twenty minutes, Kevin Devany hobbled down the floor of Cedarwood County Hospital's Psychiatric Emergency Services. He would never see the outside of the facility again.

Several hours later Brennan received a call from the resident psychiatrist at PES. Despite the written summary Brennan had submitted with the psychiatric hold document – which he concluded they never read anyway – the doctor called to find out "what we are supposed to do with him."

Brennan explained the history, and how it appeared Devany could no longer be safely housed outside in the community. His increasing anxiety turned to violence, and his behavior would not be conducive to anywhere outside the gero-psych facility.

The doctor reluctantly agreed, saying this behavior had already been exhibited in the hospital as well. He said he would be evaluated for a mental health conservatorship and – as Brennan recommended – likely be placed permanently in the gero-psych unit.

"Oh, Bobby..?" Sandra the receptionist called to Bob Foster, as he strode through the reception area of Adult Services.

"Yeah..?" Foster answered, headed for his cubicle.

"You have a phone call...a Mr. Reilly."

"Oh, yeah...?" Foster pecked, increasing his pace.

"Picking up his receiver – Foster hated headsets – he answered, "Adult Services... Bob Foster."

"Mr. Foster?" a wavering male voice spoke on the other end. "My name is Peter Reilly. My wife's name is Alice Reilly. She's forty-eight years old. We were referred to you by Dr. Field's office."

"Yes, Mr. Reilly," Foster acknowledged. "My colleague took a report from Tracy Gardner, the nurse at Dr. Field's office I've been expecting your call. What's going on?"

"You know my wife's situation then?"

"A little," said Foster. "Why don't you tell me what's happening now?"

"Well..." Reilly's voice quivered. "I just can't take it anymore. I don't know if you heard...my son has been providing care for my wife, but he broke down last week, and was hospitalized as suicidal. He's now staying with friends, and refusing to return home to take care of his mother. I don't blame him!"

"Mmmmm-hmmm..." Foster said.

"I'm at the end of my rope, Mr. Foster. My wife Alice can't – or won't – get out of bed. She says she can't walk, and never moves from bed. Every time I try to get her to move, she screams in pain. She won't let me sleep at night, and I just can't take care of her anymore."

"Tracy Gardner said she was diagnosed with conversion disorder," Foster said. "There's no physical reason why she can't walk, right?"

"Not that we know of. She used to be able to sit up in a chair, but now she can't even do that. Six months ago a psychiatrist made a home visit. She diagnosed her with conversion disorder and something to do with anxiety. She prescribed Zoloft for her, but she refused to take it. She takes numerous medications, though, including valium and other over-the-counter medications."

"I understand a nurse tried to come out to see her last week…" Foster said.

"Yes, but she wouldn't let the nurse come in. She's been begging me to give her a little more time…a couple more days, she says, to get herself together. I don't know what to do."

"I understand the doctor is concerned about bed sores…"

"Yes, she goes to the bathroom on the bed. I try to clean it up the best I can, but I can't get under her very easily to clean. She isn't very well either. It's terrible…she says if someone moves her it will kill her…she's already starting to call, just as I'm calling you…I don't know what to do…"

"Well," Foster said, "it sounds like there's no point in waiting any longer."

"What do you mean?"

"I'm gonna come to your house, and talk to your wife, and probably place her on a psychiatric hold. It sounds like she needs a hospital. If you could put whatever medications she's taking into a bag, so the paramedics can see what she's been taking, that would be helpful."

"Okay, I will," said Reilly. "I don't see any other way. I feel terribly guilty for doing this, but I just can't take care of her anymore."

"Nobody could," Foster said. "Sounds like there ain't nothing else you can do for her. She needs a hospital, and she's not willing or able to go, so we're gonna make that decision for her."

"How soon can you get here?" Reilly asked.

"Give me an hour," Foster said. "You'll be there?"

"Yes, I'll wait for you," Reilly said. "Please hurry. She's already getting upset…"

It actually took Foster about forty-five minutes to reach the Reilly's apartment in the hills of western Brystol. He called for the ambulance en route, and asked that it meet him at the Reilly home. Peter Reilly – two inches shorter than Foster with sandy gray hair, a mustache, and a little paunch – met the big social worker at the front door of the apartment building. He led Foster up the narrow stairwell to the second floor, and down the carpeted hallway to the apartment to meet Alice Reilly.

Foster estimated Alice to be about five feet, two inches tall, and to weight about 250 pounds. She lay on a cot-like bed in the living room, which otherwise appeared to be rather tidy and orderly. Peter had moved a second bed next to the cot, where he slept at night by her side. The early afternoon sun shined into the apartment, warming the peculiar smell emanating from Alice Reilly.

Alice wore a disheveled nightgown over her bloated torso, and a crumpled, stained blanket covered below her waist. Her extraordinarily swollen, apparently motionless right leg lay in a sharp angular position away from her left. Greatly overweight, her distended abdomen protruded under the insufficient material of her night garment. Brown and yellow stains streaked the sheet covering the bed, the blanket, and the nightgown.

Alice immediately started to make excuses, as if anticipating the reason for Foster's visit: "I begged Peter to give me two more days. I'm not ready to go yet."

"I'm sorry, Mrs. Reilly," said Foster. "Your doctor's office called very concerned your skin may be breaking down and becoming infected. Since you would not allow the nurse to see you last week, there's no other choice but to take you to the hospital."

"Listen…listen…!" Alice began to bargain. "I don't want to be uncooperative, I really don't…but I can't be moved! The pain is too much. Can't you give me some medication for the pain before you move me?!"

"I can't," Foster said, peering down toward her, "and I doubt the paramedics can either, but we can ask. We'll have to see what they say."

Just then the intercom buzzed, and the paramedics informed Peter the ambulance had arrived. A large-boned, sandy haired female named Laurie – dressed in her navy blue paramedic coveralls – entered the apartment a few minutes later. A muscular, similarly dressed, dark-haired male named Matt accompanied her. Foster quickly explained the situation to them, and Laurie began to examine Alice to try to determine the status of her health.

"What are you going to do!!?" Alice panicked, her face twisted in fear, as Laurie reached out a latex-gloved hand to assess Alice's right leg.

"I need to look at your leg," Laurie said, "to see what's wrong."

"Don't touch...aaahhh!" Alice screamed. "Don't touch it! I can't bear it...aaahhh!"

As Laurie felt the leg, she found the skin extremely spongy, almost as if no bone lay inside the limb at all. She found fungus between the toes, indicating the area had not been washed in many weeks. "At least I can feel a pulse," she said to Matt.

"Be careful!" Alice whimpered. "I can't stand the pain!" Peter stood behind the bed, closing his eyes, seemingly steadying himself against a wave of light-headed nausea gripping his body.

"We'll be careful, Alice," said Laurie.

"What are you doing now?" Alice screamed. "Don't hurt me!"

"I need to check the skin on your back," Laurie told her. "I'll be gentle."

Laurie needed to probe only briefly, as her expression grimaced. She excused herself, motioning for Foster and her partner to follow her into the hall.

"Her skin is really bad..." Laurie said, "...several bed sores. It doesn't look like she's moved in months..."

"Her husband said she used to sit up," said Foster, "but now she ain't able even to do that."

"Does she have a mental health diagnosis?" Matt asked.

"Apparently, a psychiatrist came out here six months ago, and diagnosed her with conversion disorder."

"What's that?" Laurie asked.

"Essentially," Foster explained, "the client converts the anxiety she feels psychologically into physical symptoms. In this case, Alice believes she can't walk, and there ain't no medical reason why."

"Well, there may be now," said Laurie. "It looks like she has been in that bed so long she can no longer move that leg. I can't tell if it's broken or simply atrophied from lack of use."

"In any case, we're gonna have to move her," Matt said. "The question is how."

"I think we're going to need some back up," Laurie said. "Why don't you call while I go talk to Alice some more?"

Matt stayed in the hallway, dialing his cell phone, while Laurie approached Alice Reilly again.

"Listen!!" Alice pleaded with Laurie again, "Could you please, please give me some pain medication?! I can't stand this pain!"

"I'm sorry, Alice," Laurie said. "I'm not a physician, and I can't give you any medication without a physician's order."

"But I'll never be able to make it without it," Alice yelled. "You won't be able to move me! It'll kill me!!"

"Alice," Foster addressed her, looking straight at her. She momentarily stopped her wailing. "There is something seriously wrong with your leg, and your skin is breaking down from laying on it so long. You won't get any better staying here, and the only way we can treat you is to take you to the hospital, where they can evaluate you, to figure out how to treat you."

"No, no…you can't," she cried, "it will hurt too much!! I can't take the pain!!"

Foster called Laurie over to him and said quietly," Those cries sound more like fear than pain. Her problem's her anxiety more than any actual injury. She's also hooked on valium, and whatever other painkiller she's taking."

"I think so," the paramedic agreed, "although that leg really concerns me."

Foster disappeared into the back bedroom to phone the hospital, to let them know Alice would be transported. The king-sized bed stood straight and creased, its staid yellow comforter covered with letters and books. Clearly, it had not been used in a very long time. "How do they live like this?" Foster muttered to himself, as he hung up the phone. "It's just amazing!"

By the time Foster returned from the back bedroom, another set of paramedics had arrived: a husky, brown-haired gentleman, and a woman in a brunette pony tail. With the appearance of additional paramedics, Alice's anxiety shot through the roof. She began to whine and plead even longer and louder. Each time a paramedic would touch her – particularly on any part of her legs – she would wail in agony. Despite all the energy pouring out of her mouth, Alice still could not – or would not – move any part of her lower body. She could not thrash or kick, but merely sobbed and begged and screamed.

Finally, the paramedics decided – given the angle of the stairwell in relation to the length of the wheeled gurney – to use the hand-held stretcher. They fixed an inflatable cushion around the right leg, to brace it against impact. Alice screamed! They fastened a vinyl restraint around Alice's body, to keep her immobile during transport. Alice Screamed louder! And when the four grabbed hold of the stained sheet beneath her, hoisting her from the bed onto the prone stretcher, she screamed the loudest and hardest of all.

Alice kept screeching, "I'm going to die!" and "You're killing me!" But the force behind her banshee shrieks revealed great distance between Alice and death's door. At one point Matt turned to Foster and said, "They should make earplugs standard issue equipment." All the while Laurie tried to calm Alice down, urging her to take deep, even breaths. Laurie's directions only agitated Alice more. Foster shook his head, as if to say, "Don't bother, she's beyond reason."

Within thirty minutes – although it seemed like hours – the paramedics had secured Alice Reilly to the stretcher, and began carrying her to the ambulance. Her screams echoes though the hall, down the stairwell, and out the front door.

"If she was really in that much pain," Matt said, "she would have passed out by now."

"It's fear," Foster reiterated. "That's really what she's screaming about."

Peter Reilly rung his hands as the ambulance doors closed behind his wife. "Believe me," Foster reassured him, "there was nothing else you could do. Alice absolutely had to go to the hospital. There's no question."

"Thank you," Peter said, closing his eyes. "I appreciate your help. I'll follow the ambulance in my car."

Bob Foster handed the psychiatric hold form to Laurie. "Pinecrest Psychiatric Hospital," he directed, "and thanks for your help."

Foster called the hospital again, to warn them about the woman about to cross their threshold.

Chapter 8
AUGUST

Patrick Brennan and Sollie Rivers drove out together on the first smoggy August Thursday afternoon, to the home of Edward and Mary Nichols. Rivers had been working with the couple for two weeks, with Mary Nichols as the primary client. Mary Nichols had been dying of throat cancer, and her husband Edward – who had a history of bipolar disorder, including several suicide attempts – found it difficult to make decisions about her care, and to provide adequate help for her during her illness. The couple – who had no children – had plenty of money. But as Mary grew more ill, Edward found it more difficult to deal with the situation emotionally. Rivers stepped in at the bequest of a minister, to help Edward make some decisions concerning the appropriate level of care for his wife.

Rivers worked with Edward to obtain help in the home for his wife. They found a hospital bed for her, and they hired an attendant to be with her when Edward could not. Nurses came to the house to monitor Mary's illness, which had fallen to the status of terminal.

Throughout the illness of his wife, Edward had exhibited signs of bipolar tendency: severe mood swings, emotional liability, tendencies toward impulsive behavior. But as his wife's illness progressed, his emotional difficulties more greatly encumbered his ability to manage day to day activities.

Finally, Mary succumbed to the cancer the previous day and went to the hospital, accompanied by Edward. She died that night. Edward spent the night in the hospital with her. Sollie Rivers figured it would be the perfect place for him. If he experienced a suicidal episode over the death of his wife, he would be in the hospital, the staff of which would be able to confine him and attend to his needs.

Unfortunately, as Rivers discovered, apparently nobody at the hospital bothered to assess Edward for suicidal ideation – as Rivers warned the night nurse – because they sent him home, the following morning. Then – of course – they called the Hotline to let Rivers know Edward came home. When Bob Foster asked the nurse on the morning shift if Edward had been assessed, she apparently responded, "Well, Mr. Nichols is not a patient in this hospital. Besides, he seemed okay to the night nurse."

"Oh, damn!" Rivers swore when Foster gave him the news. "They sent him home alone?! Don't they goddamned know anything!"

Rivers knew Edward would be heading home to his empty house for the first time. Knowing Edward's history, Rivers feared how he would react to being home alone, and questioned his ability to confront his grief over his wife's death. He called Edward as soon as the older man returned from the hospital by cab. Edward, in a very emotional voice, agreed to allow Rivers to come over and see him. Edward had made a contract with Rivers to come over and see him. He also made a contract with Rivers not to kill himself, which alleviated the social worker's fears for the moment. But Rivers nevertheless asked Patrick Brennan to come with him, not trusting what Edward might to over the long run.

Brennan stopped the Oldsmobile in a townhouse neighborhood in Maple Creek, in front of a two-story condominium with neatly trimmed lawns and standard-issue shrubbery. Edward Nichols greeted Rivers and Brennan at the door. A gray-haired, mustached man of medium height and a slight paunch, Nichols dressed in a blue satin bathrobe and thong slippers. His mussed hair appeared as if he had rubbed it roughly several times with his hand. The stubble of a beard covered his chin, and his eyes looked bleary and bloodshot. It was assumed he had not slept since he left the hospital.

"Hello, Sollie," Nichols said, his face frozen between a brave smile and a desperate frown.

"Hey, Edward," Rivers answered, taking his hand. "How are you feeling?"

"Oh, gosh…" Nichols sighed, running his hand through his hair, leading the social workers into the home. "I don't know, Sollie. It's been a pretty rough night…" he broke of his mumbling, lowered his head, and began to weep. But then he suddenly stopped himself, and attempted to pull himself together. "Can I get you gentlemen something…coffee…juice…"

"I'm okay," Rivers said.

"Nothing for me," answered Brennan.

Nichols led Rivers and Brennan to the living room, where a matching sofa and love seat ensemble nestled comfortably around a glass coffee table. Both Rivers and Brennan noticed the scotch glass perched on the table, filled with ice and what appeared to be scotch whiskey. While Rivers and Brennan sat down on the sofa, Nichols sat momentarily – and fidgeted – upon the love seat. He then bolted up, ambling over to the fireplace, where he pulled a cigarette out of his robe pocket, and lit it. He stared a few seconds at a picture on the mantel, and then wandered back to the love seat. He seemed unable to sit and relax, but rocked back and forth, very anxious. For a moment he seemed to break down again, hiding his face in his palms. But then he straightened again, fixing his jaw resolutely, puffing adamantly at the cigarette.

Sollie Rivers watched his client squirm for a few moments, and then said, "Mr. Nichols, have you been drinking?"

"Yeah…a little," Nichols answered, "…takes the edge off."

"I'm a little worried about you, Edward," Rivers continued.

"No…I'm fine…" Nichols answered quickly.

"That's unusual," Rivers said. "Most people who have been through what you've been through the last 24 hours would be a wreck."

"Well, I've sort of been preparing for…" Nichols began, but he could not finish. He once again broke down into a series of sobs, which he then fought to suppress.

"I understand you've been to see a psychiatrist. When was the last time you saw him?"

Nichols stopped, and then looked over at Rivers. "Why do you ask?"

"I think it's important you have some emotional support right now, Edward. You've been through a lot, and you need some help, some time and space to grieve."

"I haven't seen my psychiatrist for several months," Nichols said. "With my wife ill, I felt I could not afford to think about my problems, but just concentrate on my wife."

"Is there anyone you could stay with for a while, or who could stay with you, Edward? I'm a little concerned about you being left alone."

"I don't know anyone," Nichols said. "I'll be all right."

"During this illness with your wife," Patrick Brennan interjected, "have you ever thought about hurting yourself…about suicide?"

Nichols stopped, as if he had just heard something he'd been avoiding, but at the same time hoping someone would ask. He nodded slowly.

"When was the last time you thought of that?"

"I think about it a lot," he said.

"How do you think you would do it?" Rivers asked.

"What do you mean?"

"What would be your plan for committing suicide?"

Nichols paused a moment, and then said matter-of-factly, "Pills."

Brennan responded, "You mean an overdose?"

Nichols hesitated. "Yes."

"Have you ever attempted an overdose before?" Brennan asked.

Nichols paused again, searching for condemnation in the social workers' eyes. He found none. "Yes…painkillers…about two years ago, when I learned my wife had cancer. That's why I'm seeing a psychiatrist."

"Have you attempted suicide since then?" Brennan asked, being slow and deliberate in his question.

"No…but I've thought of it."

"Edward," Rivers asked now, sitting up straight, "are there any painkillers in the house now?"

Nichols paused another moment, and then nodded, "In the bathroom…they were my wife's"

"What would keep you from attempting an overdose again, Mr. Nichols?" Brennan asked.

Nichols rested his chin in his hand, which braced again his knee. Then he began to sob again. "I don't know…" he cried. "Oh, Mary…"

Brennan looked at Rivers, who nodded in silent agreement. Brennan left the room and walked out the front door. Rivers waited patiently until Nichols stopped crying.

"Edward," Rivers said, "I'm worried about you being here by yourself tonight. With your wife dying, and with your current condition, and your history of suicidal ideation, Patrick and I think it would be a good idea if you went to the hospital tonight."

"No, I'll be fine Sollie…" Nichols sniffed, fighting back the tears again, trying to be the "good soldier".

"Edward?" Rivers questioned, looking him straight in the eye.

Nichols hung his head. "You're right," he said, breaking down further. "I don't know what I'll do without my Mary…"

Edward Nichols buried his face in his hands, and sobbed deeply. Sollie Rivers sat down next to him, placing a hand on his shoulder, letting him grieve as he needed.

Meanwhile, even though the triage nurse told Brennan it might take an hour, the ambulance managed to arrive within ten minutes. Even though Edward Nichols had agreed to go to the hospital voluntarily, Brennan always worried about clients suddenly changing their minds at the hospital. With no basis to hold them against their wills, the paramedics would be forced to let them go. Brennan wrote up a psychiatric hold form, to make sure Nichols got to where he was supposed to go.

Rivers escorted the grieving Nichols to the back of the ambulance, which Nichols entered under his own power and without incident. He confessed to Rivers he knew he would need some help for a while, and he was actually glad Rivers and Brennan decided to do this. He appeared relieved that the potential decision – of whether to live or die – had been taken from his hands.

"That's okay, Edward," Rivers said, "that's why we get the big money."

The next day, Bob Foster received an update from nurse Tracy Gardner about Alice Reilly. It turned out Alice's leg indeed had been broken, but neither Peter nor Alice could say how it happened. The hospital called in a chemical dependency specialist, to assess Alice for her pain medication addiction. Reportedly Alice screamed constantly, desperately trying to keep medical personnel from touching her in any way. Her husband wanted to have her placed in a skilled nursing facility, because he simply cannot take care of her. He would be applying for government assistance for her, because the family could not afford the nursing care themselves.

Foster conveyed to the nurse he believed Peter and Alice allowed her anxiety to so completely rule their lives. She had regressed to the emotional age of an infant. She ate, she defecated, and she slept in the bed, completely reliant on others for her care and help. When she did not get what she wanted, when she was afraid, when she was mad, or when someone tried to make her do something she did not want to do, she screamed – just like an infant.

"I just don't understand how her husband could have been so blind to her condition all this time?" Foster said. "How could he let this go on all this time?"

"It's actually pretty simple," said Gardner. "The son provided almost all the care to Alice, until the stress became too much for him. The son provided a buffer for the husband, so the husband didn't have to see what was going on."

"Oh, well," Foster shrugged, "he sure has to look at it now."

Several mornings later, Donna Briar, Patrick Brennan, and Sollie Rivers sat inside

the bullpen, discussing some aspects of a case. Bob Foster wandered into the quadrangle, balancing a paper plate of some kind of food in his hand, and dangling a mug of coffee in the other. The food appeared solid, although it slid and jiggled about the plate in semi-liquid fashion. Colored primarily brown of various shades and depths, it had bits of red and chunks of white scattered about its surface. As he sat down to consume his breakfast, he realized six pairs of eyes watched him with rapt interest.

"What...? he said, as he readied his plastic fork to dig into the entrée.

"Where'd you get that?" Brennan grimaced.

"What?" Foster responded irritated.

"That thing on your place," Brennan replied.

"It's breakfast...from the cafeteria..."

"Oh...?" Rivers chimed, unable to restrain himself.

"Yeah," Foster said churlishly, "something wrong with that?"

"Oh, no...nothing," Brennan assured him.

Silence followed, as the fork prongs pierced the surface of the mass.

Rivers paused a moment, and then inquired, "So...what is it?"

"This..." Foster answered, with a mouthful, "...corned beef hash."

"...from the hospital cafeteria?" Rivers continued.

"Yeah..." Foster said. "Boy, I ain't had corned beef hash in years. My mother used to cook the meat up all day, and then she'd mix in the cabbage and the potatoes and the vegetables and the spices...it was great..." Foster maneuvered the fork to scoop another portion.

"How quaint..." Rivers said.

"Hey, Sollie," Brennan said, "did you notice they moved the Coroner's office right next to the cafeteria."

"Oh, yeah...I saw the coroner's plaque on the wall there and everything," Rivers nodded, "and I noticed the cafeteria refrigeration unit is against the same wall as the coroner's locker."

Briar shook her head, grinning, "You guys are disgusting..."

Foster raised his head slightly, and arched his eyebrow menacingly. But despite himself, he looked again at the plate before him, and poked cautiously at the hash.

"Oh, yeah," said Brennan, "but I'm sure it's mere coincidence."

"Yeah," Rivers said, "but I noticed the cook and the coroner conversing in the hall a lot. It looked like they were comparing notes on their clipboards or something. I'm sure it doesn't mean a thing, though."

"Well, y'know," Brennan went on. "I heard they had to cut the coroner's budget something fierce. They're having a hard time disposing of all those bodies. It looks awfully convenient to me."

"Hey, maybe they were comparing recipes…"

"That does it," Foster barked, rising to his feet. "I'm gonna to go eat in peace. I ain't gonna let you jerks ruin my breakfast!"

Foster stormed off for an interview room, while Rivers and Brennan chuckled away."

The next day, Patrick received a call from the gero-psychiatric unit at Cedarwood General. Keven Devany died of a cerebral hemorrhage the night before. The remainder of the account with the representative payee would be needed for the burial.

Brennan hung up the phone, and reported the news to Sollie Rivers. They each sat in silence for a moment. Then Rivers said, "Mr. Devany…"

"Yep," Brennan concluded.

"Well, that's how it goes here," Rivers suggested. "Sometimes it seems like our job is to get them to die as quietly, and with as little trouble to the community as possible"

"It took a lot of work with Mr. Devany," Brennan said.

"Yeah," Rivers agreed.

They sat in silence for a few more moments, and then Brennan returned to his desk.

"You should know…" began Chuck Corley, addressing the next Thursday's unit meeting, "…that I've received a couple of visitors over the last month. There was a line supervisor from Willet County, and another from Elk County. Our intake process is being studied by numerous adult service departments around the state, and so these supervisors came to see how we operate here."

A curious silence filled the room, as the APS staff sort of looked around, shrugging and grinning at each other.

"Actually," continued Corley, "this unit is becoming something of a model for the rest of the state. No other APS unit is so responsive on such a wide variety of issues as Cedarwood County."

More silence ensued.

"Doesn't anyone have any reaction to this information?" Corley inquired.

Emma Hayes looked at Rhonda Pagan, who glanced at Sollie Rivers, who nodded toward the senior staffer, Bob Foster. "Well, Chuck, you know we've talked about this subject before. There may be a damned good reason why other counties don't do what we do."

"In most counties, you're lucky if you don't get an answering machine," quipped Donna Briar. "Having three full time workers to answer phones is unheard of."

"And other counties limit their responses to strictly Adult Protective Services functions: mandated reports of elder or dependent adult abuse or neglect," said Hayes. "They don't go running out every time someone has a bad feeling about someone else. We respond to a far greater range of issues than anyone else. Sometimes I wonder, in the long run, if we are actually being helpful or detrimental to the community."

'How do you mean?" Corley quizzed. "I know we've each talked about this in various forums before, but I think it's an important discussion."

"Sometimes I wonder what the residents would do if we didn't exist," said Brennan. "I mean, I wonder if they'd be able to figure out a lot of this stuff on their own, if they knew they could not rely on 'the government' to fix things."

"Our relationship with the public is very co-dependent," said Hayes. "Like Patrick said, instead of calling upon their own resources and capabilities, they seem to automatically want to rely on us to solve their problems. The truth is, we can't solve very many of their problems. Only they can, and yet sometimes I think our presence takes that option away for them."

"The other thing that happens," said Foster, "is it shelters the larger community from the mess that exists in it. With APS intervening among the homeless, the disabled, the derelicts, the alcoholics, the drug addicts, the demented, the impoverished, the disenfranchised, we act as a filter for the larger society. They don't have to recognize it or acknowledge it because they know we'll deal with it for them. If they don't see the problems, they don't feel any responsibility for them and – by the way – they don't feel like they should pay extra taxes to pay for these programs."

"What I envision as our role…" said Hayes…"is that of the Dutch boys, with their fingers in the levee. We keep the waves of the underprivileged and disadvantaged from overwhelming the community. In Jungian terns, we're paid for protecting the shadow of society, so society doesn't have to."

"But at the same time," said Rivers, "we start making decisions about our clients based on the comfort zone of the community. Instead of allowing an elderly client to die in his own home, like he wants, we strap him in a gurney and haul him off to the hospital as a gravely disabled because his nervous nelly neighbor somehow can't bear the thought of someone dying next door or something. We're not going to stop the person from dying, but if a neighbor complains – especially a neighbor who plays cards with some government official – we make sure the neighbor doesn't have to be bothered by the discomfort."

"There is no doubt," said Foster, "very often – especially in these so-called self neglect cases – the client is the community, and it's the community's needs we end up addressing."

"It is very clear," Briar added, "I think we all take a great deal of pride in the work we do. We seem to be able to do far more things - and apparently do them far better – than any other APS unit in the state. The question is: should we be doing all we do? In the long run, is it benefiting the community, or simply enabling their dependence."

"I empathize with a lot you are saying," Corley said, "and some of it I agree with. It is never an easy question to answer: when does helping become enabling? This is a question we will continue to struggle with, and I think it is important we bring it up for discussion now and again, to express what we are thinking and feeling."

This time, everyone seemed to nod in consensus.

"I appreciate your input," added Corley. "That's it for today."

Chapter 9
SEPTEMBER

APS units face an ongoing tug-of-war between the idea of personal safety, and the concept of personal independence. Like Children's Protective Services (CPS), APS face clients trapped in very hazardous and abusive situations. APS staff has some responsibility to ensure the safety of those clients. But unlike the young clients of CPS, APS clients are adults who have guaranteed civil rights and responsibilities concerning their own lives. In CPS, the clients virtually have no rights, and their welfare and safety are based on the determination of how well their parents can provide for and protect them. It is always assumed the children do not have the legal rights, the responsibility, or the ability to decide where and how they shall live. For adults, however, it is much different. As long as they are deemed mentally competent, there is very little APS workers can do to protect these people from themselves and their relationships. There are last resorts – such as a psychiatric hold, and ultimately conservatorship – which APS can use to protect people from their own harmful tendencies. Yet these measures can only be enlisted often after considerable deliberation, in the midst of situations rarely – if ever – clear cut.

In Cedarwood Adult Services, subtle lines existed between workers who lean toward a priority of personal safety, and those who favor personal independence. In general, the workers who are personally responsible for the clients' welfare and safety – Deputy Public Guardians and Conservatorship Investigators – make personal safety much more of a priority. The social workers and nurses of APS, however, tended to view personal independence with preeminence. The most possible help in the least restrictive manner remained the APS worker's primary goal. APS workers recognized that, by and large, most of their clients would readily give up adequate food, clothing, shelter, hygiene, and medical care before they are willing to give up the individual freedom to determine the course of their lives.

Chuck Corley, Patrick Brennan, and Emma Hayes gathered in an interview room on a hot and humid Wednesday, to consult about the latest of Emma Hayes' cases. In this one, Ari Davis – chomping furiously at the bit – had become involved. It concerned a sixty-four year old multiple sclerosis patient named Ruby Rosetti. She lived in a house in upper Corning with her husband, Arnold. Non-ambulatory, manipulative, and totally dependent on her husband for her care and provision, she had nonetheless been referred to APS eight separate times, for accusing her own husband of abuse or neglect.

Arnold had completely subjugated his own will and needs to those of his wife. Before leaving early in the morning to attend to his janitorial supply business, the sixty-eight year old Arnold would physically carry his wife in his arms to the bathroom. He would return her to her bed, leaving a phone on her night table, which she could use in an emergency. He would work all morning, then return home to fix a meal for Ruby and himself. He would stay home and attend to Ruby's beck and call until dinner. Then he would gather Ruby in his arms, carry her out to the car, and take her out to dinner.

Upon feeding her – literally, since she had limited use of her hands – he would carry her back to the car, drive back to the house, and physically hoist her back into the house, and into her bed. Although he freely admitted to his frustration with the situation, an actual incident of physical abuse had not yet been sustained.

Though Arnold had been repeatedly advised to hire someone to help him in the home – something the Rosetti's could readily afford – Ruby would regularly countermand his provision. She would either fire the attendant procured, or complain infernally about the money used to hire the attendant. As usual, Arnold would be browbeaten into submission, forced – by some undetermined power – once again to provide the care himself.

Emma Hayes had been called into the case because Ruby started calling 911 on a regular basis, accusing her husband of physically abusing and neglecting her. She would tell the police Arnold had slapped and pushed her, but neither injury would be detectable – until this last incident. She would accuse him of neglecting her, leaving her alone in the morning while he went to work; yet she would refuse to allow him to hire the help she needed. Emotionally and cognitively resigned, Arnold stood at her command; Ruby wanted him physically in her presence at all times as well. Although in his frustration Arnold repeatedly blurted out threats to divorce and abandon her, Ruby seemed to know he would remain incapable of doing so. As dependent and enmeshed as she was with him, he was equally so with her. Finally, one evening Arnold threw her across the bed in a fit of frustration, leading to the latest APS referral.

In addition to Ruby's physical needs, the home had continually fallen into a deeper state of disrepair. As her disability worsened, Ruby had developed into something of a pack rat, hoarding newspapers, and refusing to allow her husband or her children to throw anything out.

Anticipating the Rosetti's resistance, Emma had sought the intervention of Ari Davis who, during her assessment for conservatorship, told the Rosetti's if they did not allow help in the home, she would file a petition for conservatorship, and perhaps even arrange for Ruby to be removed from the home as a danger to herself, and a gravely disabled adult. She also threatened to report them to the Environmental Health Division, whom Davis said could possible close the house as uninhabitable. Through her threats, Davis had induced the Rosetti's to agree to hire help.

Although an attendant from Lifecare Home Services began coming to the home a week previous, the agency had called Hayes this particular morning, saying the Rosetti's had refused to allow her into the house. Much to Hayes' chagrin, Davis had drawn a line for the Rosetti's, in an attempt to dissuade them from their dysfunctional behavior. The Rosetti's – once again – had crossed the line, and now it remained for the APS unit to respond.

"So, what do you want to do?" Corley asked Hayes, once Brennan had taken his seat at the small conference table.

"Well, I wouldn't have started making threats," Hayes said, rolling her eyes.

"Me neither," Brennan said. "That's the clear path to a power struggle, which never works."

"Well, Ari has her own style, "said Corley, "and sometimes, it provides an advantage."

"So, what can we do?" Hayes asked. "Ruby is very alert and oriented, and has capacity to make decisions: her doctor has said this all along."

"Is she in danger when she's home by herself?" Brennan asked.

"Technically, I suppose," Hayes explained. "Like, if there was a fire, she would not be able to get out, although she could certainly call 911 – as we are all quite aware. Besides, they have been operating like this for years."

"Doesn't sound like an immediate danger to me," Brennan suggested.

"But we can't keep doing this," Corley said. "This couple has plenty of money, and the situation would be easily fixable. But she refuses to take the appropriate steps, and she continues to call 911, which is upsetting the authorities."

"Well, Ari knows about the situation, and she has called Hiram Zinder at Environmental Health to determine if the house is postable. If it is, there may be grounds for a psychiatric hold."

"I'm never anxious to do a hold," Brennan said, "but even if we brought her in, would the hospital keep her? From what you've told me, Em, the doctor thinks she's competent. She has no acute medical need. On what basis would they keep her in the hospital?"

"I don't know," Hayes responded.

"What is it that keeps her from hiring help, Emma?" Corley asked.

"She is completely dependent on her husband," said Hayes, "and apparently wants to stay that way. Her dependence seems to touch some strain of guilt within him, which keeps him from saying no to her. She is bed bound and non-ambulatory, but her disability keeps him completely in her control. She completely rules the roost – no matter what accusations she makes of him."

"And I guess he would never admit to being unable to deal with it…?"

"No way…!" Hayes said. "It's, like, his sacred mission, and his eternal punishment as well."

"How many referrals have we gotten on these two?" Corley asked.

'I think this is the ninth," Hayes answered.

"Is she physically worse off now?"

"She seems to be able to do less for herself, yes," Hayes agreed.

"What about mentally..?"

"Cognitively she seems about the same, but she is more anxious, wanting to be more controlling and isolating, and she's drawing her husband in as well."

"How is his health?"

"He's obviously stressed by all this, and he has some heart problems. But he still seems pretty strong. I mean, he can still carry her to the car, after all these years. But now with this last incident, it's obvious his stress is reaching a critical level, and he is beginning to lash out physically against her."

"Ari's already on her way out to the house?"

"Yep, and she's bringing Hiram with her."

"Well, I don't know what's going to happen," Corley said, "but you two might as well get out there. If you decide to bring her in, Patrick, let me know. I'll make sure Marlene calls the hospital, and directs them to keep her there."

"Should we bring Rhonda?" Hayes asked.

"You may as well…I think we're going to need all the input we can get."

"Oh, good…" Brennan said, "…a bloody field trip!" As Hayes and Brennan charged out of Corley's office, Brennan found Rhonda Pagan about to sit down at her desk. "Hey, Rhonda," he quipped, "doing anything special?"

"Uh…" she hesitated, grimacing. "Why do you want to know?"

"We're going on a field trip," Hayes told her. "Me and Patrick are going to meet Ari and Hiram, out at the Rosetti house."

"Is that the MS patient Ari was talking about?"

"You've heard of them," Brennan said. "They're refusing home health. Ari's got a head of steam up after them. Hiram's going to check out the house. We're going to see what we can do about it. You might as well come along and evaluate her medical condition, while we're at it."

"Chuck thought it would be good for you to come along," Hayes added.

"Oh, well," Rhonda shrugged, "apparently I've nothing better to do, then…"

Hayes and Brennan briefed Pagan on the way to the Rosetti's place. The public health nurse remained confused as to exactly why she had been summoned out there, since it did not sound like there would be any acute medical issues to address."

"I think it's a matter of 'just in case'," Hayes told her. "We are looking for some way to break this stalemate we have here. If we can find any medical reason, it would add to our efforts."

Arielle Davis waited as the Rosetti's front porch like a leashed bloodhound. Hiram Zinder of the county Environmental Health Department accompanied Davis. Zinder came to determine the habitability of the home. Davis told the arriving trio she'd knocked on the door several times, but there'd been no response. "I don't know if Arnold is in there," Davis reported, "but if Ruby is there by herself, she certainly couldn't answer the door."

"Well, what are we going do now?" Brennan said. "We've no authority to break into the house."

"Why don't I call the Corning police," Hayes said, reaching for the cell phone. "They've had numerous contacts with this couple, and they may have an idea of what to do."

Meanwhile, Chuck Corley took a call in his office, decorated in the Japanese culture motif he found so fascinating. Corley gazed at the rice paper sketching which covered the wall behind him, while a sitting, porcelain Buddha sat on the edge of his desk. Brightly colored paper lanterns dangled from the ceiling, while a freshly raked sand tray rested upon the shelves behind his desk. Corley had taken it upon himself to study and immerse himself in the Japanese culture, and had visited the island nation several times. Corley apparently derived the dignity and serenity which exemplified his life from the study of the East Asian culture.

"Good morning, Chuck here," he answered his phone.

"Is this Chuck Corley?" a male voice said.

"Yes it is. Can I help you?"

"Hey, Chuck, how's it going?" the man answered. "I was referred to you by the office of Ronald Morley, the county manager. My name is Jim Willis, and I am an agent for Carlton and Madsen, Real Estate Developers. We've run into situation which Morley's office said you can help us with."

"I'll do what I can," Corley replied.

"Good…the thing is this: we're working on a new development in Roger's Park, a shopping center which is going up in the west end of town…it'll stimulate the economy, provide jobs; really help out the community. We've been trying to arrange this project for several years, finally getting the okay from city hall last year."

"Yes…?" Corley responded.

"Well, we've run into a little snag: there's this old woman living in a spot on the very corner where we are planning to build this mini-mall. The rest of the neighbors have already come to terms with us, but this one refuses to leave. She seems real unreasonable, kind of holed up in this old house of hers – really crazy. We've made her a very reasonable offer for her property, but she refused to move. The city can confiscate the property under eminent domain, but after talking with the county manager's office, they suggested I call you."

"Well, what can I do for you, Mr. Willis?"

"Morely's office suggested we ask you to send out a social worker to evaluate this woman, and that you could take her to the hospital."

"Well, possibly…depending on the situation, and what her status is, and if she appeared to be in danger of some sort…"

"Well, I'd say losing your home is a pretty dangerous situation…particularly if you don't need to…wouldn't you, Chuck?"

"Could be…" Corley said, standing up to close the door of his office. "Why don't you give me a little more information…"

"Great, Chuck," Willis said. "I really appreciate this."

Fortunately for Hayes and company, the town of Corning was rather small, quiet, and homey, enabling the city police officers to pay additional personal attention to the residents. Emma Hayes spoke to an Officer Ken Springhorn, explaining the situation. Springhorn said he knew the Rosetti's, and would be out right away."

Meanwhile, Arielle Davis grew increasingly anxious. She felt determined if she found Ruby Rosetti home by herself – after she had warned the Rosetti's to hire an attendant while Arnold was away – there would be grounds to take her to the hospital against her will. "I'm going around back," she said.

"Isn't that breaking and entering?" Patrick cautioned her.

"Not if the door's open," Davis asserted,

Ari Davis marched down the leaf-strewn brick front porch, and wandered over to the back gate. The gate led through a small walkway hemmed in on either side by ivy hedges. It ended in the back yard, which featured a large swimming pool surrounded by the cement deck. Clusters of oak leaves floating in the pool suggested the length of time since the Rosetti's actually used it. Beyond the pool a dry, brown lawn stretched to the wooden planks of the fence. There had probably been a time when the back yard rang with the sound of family life; now it lay barren and unused.

Davis climbed up the back steps, and pushed open the sliding glass door, opening to a gold drape blocking the entry way. "Hello," she called, in the sweet, innocent voice which so often kept her from trouble, by disarming any potential objectors. With no answer forthcoming, she wandered back to Ruby's bedroom, where she found her lying in bed, awake but unmoving. Surrounding the queen-sized bed lay piles and piles of clothing and newspapers, extending back to and filling the closet, the dresser, the vanity, and most of the floor. Davis shook her head in disbelief, and then said, "Are you by yourself, Mrs. Rosetti?"

"No, my husband is going to be right back. He just went to get some things at the store."

"I thought you were going to hire some help, so you wouldn't be here by yourself."

"We're going to…just as soon as we can…"

David continued. "Lifecare called saying you refused to let the attendant in this morning…" She heard a knock at the door. "I'll be right back."

Davis marched down the hall toward the door. The light fixture in the hall ceiling had been removed, and a dank and grimy film covered the hall carpet. Davis passed a bathroom which was almost as cluttered as the bedroom, with papers stacked along the walls and inside the bathtub. Davis passed the dining room- living room complex, which also appeared dusty and cluttered. She finally opened the front door.

Hiram Zinder, Patrick, Emma, and Rhonda had been joined by two uniformed police officers from the Corning police. Davis let them in, and then all fanned out to begin to examine the house and the client. Patrick and Rhonda walked back to Ruby's bedroom, while Emma and Ari examined the front room.

Brennan spoke briefly with Rosetti. Although she could not sit by herself, she could respond clearly and lucidly to all his questions. Oriented to date, time, place, and circumstance, she knew her health situation, the name of her doctor, the last time she'd seen him. She could identify her children from the photos on her desk, and stayed focused on the conversation. She knew her date of birth and social security number. She seemed to understand the risks of staying home by herself, but she could reach the phone – she certainly knew how to call 911 – and she accurately stated nothing bad had happened so far.

While Brennan examined her cognitively, Rhonda Pagan conducted a brief physical assessment. Taking her blood pressure, monitoring her pulse, checking her skin for breakage or ulcers, Pagan could find not immediate reason for medical intervention.

In the meantime, Emma Hayes and Ari Davis searched through the front of the house, surveying the clutter and mess. The kitchen, actually, seemed the most stable of the quarters. Although there were some dirty dishes in the sink, the counter remained generally clear, and fairly clean – although there seemed to be a layer of grease lining most things. The same could not be said of the adjacent living room. Like in the bedroom: clothes and envelopes covered most of the furniture. Towers of newspapers teetered on tables and the floor, and other documents as well as scores of dishes and glasses lay motionless around the room.

"How can they live like this?" Davis sighed.

"How can they live with MS, and their marriage?" Hayes countered.

Before long, Zinder reentered the living room, heading straight for Davis. Hayes drew closer to listen. "There certainly is a lot of clutter, newspapers, and other combustibles which create a fire hazard. Also, several of the electrical fixtures are exposed, which would add to the hazard. However, the plumbing works – even if it does not appear to be used very often – and the central heating is operable. I don't see any overt signs of rodents. It certainly needs work, but I couldn't declare it uninhabitable at this point. What I can do is issue a warning letter, requiring then to make certain improvements within any given time, Perhaps that would motivate them to clean this place up a little."

Davis waggled her head in frustration, while Hayes conversed with Zinder. Suddenly, Arnold Rosett burst through the door, livid at the intrusion into his home.

"What are you people doing here?" Rosetti exclaimed, striding straight up to Ari Davis, with whom he had wrangled before. Davis met him eye to eye, declaring, "You wife is not safe here. We told you to get some help in the home for her, but you didn't do it. Lifecare told us you refused to let the attendant in, and now we have to figure out whether we can continue to leave her here.

"I can take care of her," Rosetti snorted. "I've been doing it all my life."

"Well, from the looks of things here," Davis retorted, "you haven't been doing it very well!"

Red faced, Rosettin lunged toward Davis, shouting, "What right do you have to do this...coming into my home like this...what is this, Nazi Germany?"

Officer Springhorn stepped in between Rosetti and the Deputy Public Guardian. "Come on now, Arnold," he said. "You know we've been through all this before. I've been out here two or three times myself. You've got to get some more help here. It just isn't safe."

"Well, what am I supposed to do, Ken?" Rosetti said, sitting down on a stool next to the kitchen counter. "Every time I try to spend some money to help her, she complains we're spending too much money. I told her I would take care of her, and I need to keep my promise."

"But it's too much for you," Hayes offered. "It would be too much for anyone to do alone. And the fact that your wife keeps sabotaging your efforts to help her makes it even worse..."

"I know..." Rosetti reluctantly agreed, as he glanced around the disheveled room. "I know..."

Patrick Brennan just then emerged from the back room. "This woman is very clear and lucid," he informed the gathered. "She understands the situation, and she understands the possible consequences, and seems willing to face them. The only thing is, she also doesn't seem to be realistic about how much she can afford to spend on help. She also seems to believe Mr. Rosetti can take care of her himself, without any help. It's like when you defend your own family or religion to others, but do nothing but argue and squabble among yourselves."

"But I can take care of her," Rosetti resumed the stand. "Who the hell are you, anyway?"

"I'm Patrick Brennan," he replied. "I'm here to determine whether your wife should go to a hospital, or if she's safe to be here."

"We cannot leave her like this," Ari Davis moaned, shaking her head in defiant determination.

"Well, we can't take her in, either," Hayes reiterated. "We don't have the basis."

"I can take care of her myself," Rosetti interjected. "I can get someone to come in a clean the house up. I don't need help, and I don't need you social workers meddling in my affairs."

"Well, Mr. Rosetti," said Brennan, "even though your wife seems cognitively intact, she does not seem to have the best judgment in these matters. From the looks of the situation – and just from the reality of the level of care she needs – I'd say this is an awful lot for you to take on yourself."

"Well, I can do it," Arnold Rosetti declared, at the same time rubbing a sweaty hand over his exhausted face.

"No you can't, Dad," a feminine voice declared from across the room. Everyone's eyes turned to watch a tall, brown-haired woman in her thirties enter through the front doorway. Her face resembled Ruby Rosetti, and she wore a stylish business outfit, as if she had just come from an office.

"I'm Darleen Taylor," she introduced herself.

"You're the Rosetti's daughter?" Patrick asked.

"Yes," she said, extending her hand to Brennan.,"we've been after my father to get help for mom for months, but he refuses. He has some kind of guilt of something, like he'd be abandoning her if he doesn't do it all himself."

"Darleen, please…" Arnold said, trying to quiet his daughter.

"Come on, dad," she said, placing an arm on his shoulder. "Look at you. Your face is red, you're breathing hard. You're exhausted by all this. Mom won't let you get the help you need to take care of her. She's boxing you into a corner, and I know you're frustrated by it all. Frankly, I'm surprised you haven't tried to punch her lights out years ago. These people are trying to help you, just as much as they are trying to help mom."

"Mr. Rosetti," Brennan said, "it seems your wife has unfairly laid the entire monumental job of caring for her on your shoulders. If you say you are no long able to take care of her, I can take her to the hospital as a gravely disabled adult. They can evaluate her, determine what level of care she needs, and perhaps work with her to learn to accept that the kind of care she needs requires more than one person. In the meantime, while she's in the hospital, you could work to clean up the house. Perhaps, with the proper amount of help, she'll be able to come back here."

"Sure, Dad," Darleen said, moving closer and placing another arm around his shoulder. "Rick and I can help. We can get a bin, and really clean up this place."

"But she depends on me," Rosetti said, taking his daughter's hand, looking into her eyes with tears in his own.

"You're not abandoning her," Emma Hayes spoke quietly. "You are taking steps to make sure she gets the best care she needs, and to take care of yourself as well. If you destroy yourself in the midst of caring for her, what good will it do?"

"Come on, Arnold," Officer Springhold urged, "we don't want to have to keep coming out here."

Arnold Rosetti said nothing. He slumped his shoulders, and lay his nodding head against his daughter's hip. Tears began falling form his eyes, as Darlene held him close comforted him. "It's okay, Dad," she said. "It's going to be okay."

Brennan immediately separated himself from the rest of the group, and called Corley to inform him of the decision.

"I remember in the psych hold training," he told Corley, "one thing they said is if the family wants the client brought in, you should bring her in. Based on her own mental status, Ruby Rosetti would not be holdable. But given the circumstances, with the consent of the daughter – who has convinced the father, at least for the moment – I think we can do it. If nothing else, it'll give him a few days of respite."

"Good," Corley said.

"Now, the hospital has been informed of our little plot, right?"

"Yes," Corley said. "Marlene has advised the director of the hospital. They're aware of the situation, and they are prepared to keep her there as long as Ari is going to follow her."

"Knowing Ari, that could be a long time," Brennan said.

"Yes, I know," Corley said.

"We had a pretty good stalemate going here, Chuck," Brennan said. "Ari was sure she should go, Emma was sure she couldn't, and I wasn't sure what to do. If the daughter hadn't shown up, I don't know what would've happened."

"Well, it sounds like it worked out."

"Yeah, I'll see you later."

Brennan then called PES, and requested the ambulance. Fortunately, the day appeared to be a fairly light one for both psychiatric emergency and the paramedics. The ambulance arrived within fifteen minutes, and the paramedics immediately wheeled the gurney back to Ruby Rosetti's bedroom.

Within a few minutes, the gurney reemerged, Ruby Rosetti secured atop it. All along the ride to the waiting ambulance, Ruby pleaded with Arnold to leave her in the home, as Darleen reassured her that this would be the best thing. But as soon as the gurney approached the ambulance outside, the pleading stopped, and the paramedics quietly loaded her into the ambulance.

"It's amazing," Brennan whispered to Hayes and Pagan, as they all watched the procession from the driveway. "So often I see the resignation, especially when the clients – on some level – know that this is probably the best going for them."

"Yeah, but I still hate to do it," Hayes whispered back.

"Yeah, I know," Brennan said. "But, it's a bloody lucky thing that daughter showed up. I really wasn't sure what I was going to do."

"Luck had nothing to do with it," Pagan pointed out. "I heard Emma leave Darleen a message just before we left the office."

Emma smiled. "I hoped she would get the message. After talking with her before, I figured she might be able to influence Arnold the way the rest of us couldn't."

"Emma," Patrick beamed, "You're amazing!"

Brennan handed the psychiatric hold form to the paramedics. Ari Davis eased over to Arnold Rosetti, telling him, "It's for the best. This will give you time to rest, clean up the house, and set the situation at home up that she can come back."

Arnold Rosetti nodded, tears welling up in his eyes. His daughter joined at his side, took him by the arm, and led him back into the house.

The Rosetti case illustrated the difference between cognitive incompetence and relational enmeshment and dysfunction – as Ari Davis discovered in the course of the conservatorship investigation. Separately, and by themselves, Ruby and Arnold Rosetti presented as calm, reasonable people. But together, they simply could not function appropriately for either of them. They almost took on the lifelong roles of the disabled tyrannical queen, and doleful but resentful servant. Despite Ari's intricate documentation of the way which Arnold could not provide care for his wife, the county's legal counsel finally determined it would be too difficult to demonstrate the mental incompetence of both parties. Unless it could be shown, the judge would never grant the conservatorship authority to the Public Guardian. In the end, the Public Guardian dropped the conservatorship petition.

Ruby Rosetti spent about two weeks in the hospital, then spent a month in a residential care home. Finally, through, she returned to the care of her husband.

Although it opposed the course Ari Davis would have chosen, ultimately the APS intervention proved positive. Since Ruby Rosetti's return home, there had been no further incidents of 911 calls. Darleen and her husband Rick managed to help Arnold clear away the clutter, and hired an agency to give the home a good cleaning. Lifecare Home Care sent an attendant in for three hours each morning, allowing Arnold to have time to go to his office for half the day.

It is possible despite the dysfunction, the Rosetti's could finally see their best alternative would be to alter their home lifestyle to fit the needs of both Ruby and Arnold.

Chapter 10
OCTOBER

"We got a hot one, guys," Sollie Rivers said as he found a seat in the Bullpen.

"What's up, Sollie?" Patrick asked, whirling in his chair.

"Oh, boy...we've stepped into it this time!" Rivers exclaimed, fidgeting in his chair like a third grader at a movie. Used to gauging Rivers level of histrionics, Foster and Briar figured an extraordinary situation had emerged. They readily turned to listen to Rivers, who fiddled with his tie while he talked.

"Chuck tells me to go out and evaluate this woman who lives in Rogers Park. An agent for a real estate developer was referred to us by the County Manager's office, no less, because supposedly there was this crazy old woman who does not want to move out of her house to make room for a mini-mall they want to put up. They say they've made her a very generous offer to relocate, but she's crazy and she's not cooperating. Chuck is sending me out to decide if she's holdable."

"Yeah...?" Foster queried, his eyebrow raised.

"Well, it turns out this woman is Japanese-America. She's 80 years old, and she was placed in an internment camp in Arizona with her family when she was thirteen. She owns a two-bedroom house with a nice little garden, which pretty much makes up her entire world. She owns the house so she doesn't pay rent. She shops, goes to the bank every once in a while, and spend most of the rest of her time in her home. She even wears one of those wide-brimmed sun hats when she works in the garden. She's never bothered anyone in her life."

"Sounds like she's culturally challenged," Foster said. "She lives within her own pre-arranged world, and never gets too far beyond it."

"Exactly," Rivers concurred. "She was telling me how she used to cross over a little dirt road to get to the market. Now the dirt road is the main highway through the county.

"So, let me guess…" Brennan stated sarcastically, "she's not holdable."

"No where near it," Rivers chided. "Guess what else? The so-called generous offer the city offered her to move: $180,000."

"What?" Briar exclaimed. "Are they crazy?"

"I guess so," said rivers, "or really cheap. There's no way she's going to be able to find anything else close to her current house for eighty thousand. No wonder she doesn't want to move."

"She doesn't sound crazy at all," Foster said. "She sounds pretty sharp, actually."

"She is," said Rivers. "She's just, like you say, culturally challenged. She's never had anything to do with government or real estate agents or anyone…she just wants to live her quiet, simple life."

"Bloody hell…" Brennan squawked.

"Yeah, damned developers…" Rivers fumed. "They want us to do the dirty work for them, and they enlisted Morley's help to do it. It makes it real easy for them if they can get her hospitalized as incompetent."

"Sounds like a poignant human interest feature for the local news," Foster suggested through his bifocals.

"I thought of that," Rivers said, "but Chuck says we can't risk getting caught in the middle between the county manager and the woman. I suggested we turn this over to a private advocate – like Cedarwood Paralegal Services – to defend this woman.

"Good idea," Briar said.

"They could get the house appraised – independently – and lobby for a decent price for the house so she can get something somewhere else. The advocate can use the option of media exposure as leverage. The last thing the county manager and the developer needs with this thing is bad press. My understanding is it's taken them years to convince the city of the development. Imagine if a story of how the county forced a former WWII internee out of her home, the government making her homeless for the second time in her life. The press would eat it up!"

"Here, Sollie," Briar said, handing him a card from her roll-a-deck file. "This is an attorney at Cedarwood Paralegal Services. She loves cases like this, particularly involving people of color. She loves to go after the establishment for the benefit of the poor. She'll know how to handle this."

"You're so good, Donna," Rivers smiled. "I'll call her."

"Tell her I said Hi", said Briar.

Two days later on an unusually warm October afternoon, Sollie Rivers and Bob Foster climbed up the carpeted stairwell of the small apartment complex in Brystol. Donna Briar had received an anonymous report of an elderly man named Edgar Bell, slowly wasting away by himself in his apartment. The referent had told Briar there had been a friend who occasionally would help Bell, but that friend would no longer be available. The referent described Bell as seventy-eight, extremely thin, rarely arising from his bed.

As Rivers and Foster climbed the stairwell, they could feel the temperature of the building rise appreciatively. "Smell that?" Rivers said, sniffing the air as he reached the top of the stairs.

"It gets worse as we go up the stairs," Foster observed. "I'm sure it's mere coincidence…"

"Whew!" Rivers' head shook as he approached apartment #238. "This must be the place."

The apartment door stood ajar by about a third, as if someone had left but would be returning again right away. Rivers knocked on the door frame, and then slowly pushed the door completely open. Both Rivers and Foster winced as the hot air from the apartment flooded the hallway. "Ugghh…!" Foster exclaimed. "It's like sardines…barf…and ammonia."

"Edgar Bell?" Rivers called. The social workers waited briefly, and then Rivers called again. "Edgar?"

They entered the apartment, turning left to tour through the rancid kitchen. A small hill of filthy plastic plates and aluminum pots formed within the moldy sink, as grease and food crumbs clung to both the counters and the linoleum floor. Empty bottles of wine and vodka stood upright, or tumbled among the debris. Rivers led Foster through the kitchen to the dining table, which supported its own mountain of unopened mail, disheveled newspapers, and crumpled towels. Foster picked up a couple of the envelopes. "Here's a social security check from this month," he said, "and an electric bill. These things ain't being paid!"

Matted shorts and stringy underwear hung from the coffee table, and the wooden rocking chair of the living room. A variety of stains, from an unimaginable array of substances, colored the apartment carpet. The profound stench of various bodily fluids permeated the air, as Foster forced open the cob-webbed, corner window.

"Mr. Bell?" Rivers called again. Hearing no response, Rivers whispered to Foster, "God, Bob, what if he's dead or something?"

A chill spread from Rivers' spine to Foster's. "I was just thinking the same thing," he said.

Rivers and Foster braved the hallway leading to the rear of the apartment. They peaked inside the bathroom, where they viewed the bottom of the bathtub, which had turned virtually black with mold. They continued down the hallway until it ended, at the threshold of the lone bedroom, darkened from the sun by a tattered shade.

"This must be him," Rivers pointed. Foster peered in to find a gaunt, aged figure spread-eagle on his back on a sheet-less mattress. The remnants of a solitary, shredded cover lay on one edge of the mattress. An extensive wet stain spread on the mattress underneath the standing frame. The bedroom reeked worse than the rest of the apartment. Foster gasped, "Ooops", as he assumed his worst fear, but then relaxed as he heard the feint snore, and could detect the labored rising and falling of the old man's chest. "Good", Foster whispered, "it ain't a corpse."

Rivers pointed to the gallon jug of wine sitting next to a glass tumbler on the cluttered beside table. "I should have known", Rivers shook his head.

Both social workers noticed the wrinkled skin clinging loosely to the frail bone. On Bell's right elbow, a rubber band dug into and around what appeared to be a wound of some sort; as if nothing else resembling a bandage could be found by the old man.

Rivers leaned forward and called, "Edgar Bell? Edgar..?!"

The old man snorted a grumble as he feebly attempted to awaken, but then fell back into a snoring stupor. Refraining from touching the aged wretch, Sollie Rivers shook the bed vigorously as he called louder, "Edgar! Wake up!"

Bell shook his head and his eyes fluttered open. If he had been strong enough, he might have bolted out of bed. Instead, he merely raised his grizzled jowls above his wet and tattered pillow.

"Hummermph", the old man muttered, as he attempted to focus his eyes.

"Edgar," Rivers called again. "I'm a social worker from the county. Somebody called us saying you need some help. Are you okay?"

"Wha…wha…?" Bell blurted.

"Edgar…what happened to your place?"

Foster left the room to allow Rivers to question the old man. He roamed about the apartment trying to get some more information about the shell of the man left in the bed. Foster found a check book register on a pile of papers at the foot of a moth-eaten couch. He thumbed through the register, discovering a hodge-podge of entries and attempts at arithmetic. Even if he managed somehow to get his bills paid, Foster concluded, Mr. Bell probably had no idea of the balance of his accounts.

Foster also discovered what appeared to be retirement checks from United Airlines.

Perhaps Bell had been a mechanic or a ticket manager, Foster guessed. Foster found several similar check envelopes, plus bills for the utilities, the phone, and mail orders. It became clear Bell had not been able to manage his finances for several months, and Foster began to wonder how he managed to keep himself from being evicted. He surmised the anonymous referent may have had something to do with it.

Foster wandered back to the kitchen, instinctively inspecting the refrigerator. An empty bottle of Chablis rested on its side next to a lone can of Budweiser. A jar of pickles, a few condiments, and a Chinese food container Foster avoided with all caution, comprised the sum of the contents.

Sollie Rivers joined Foster in the kitchen. "He's drinking himself to death," Rivers stated without a doubt. "He's been drinking all morning, and he couldn't tell me the last time he's eaten. He said something about some friend helping him to pay his bills."

"No one's paid any bills in a long time, Sollie. "Foster said. "Whoever might have been helping him out once ain't doin' it no more."

"The referent…" Rivers quizzed.

"That's my guess…" Foster agreed.

"Well, this guy's pretty out of it…" Rivers concluded. "He doesn't know what day it is, what time it is, even where he is…whoa…"

Rivers turned to notice a bent, trembling figure hobbling slowly up the hall. Upright – or as upright as the codger would likely ever be – Edgar Bell's disfigurement became much more apparent. Malnourishment had ravaged his frame, and a gray pallor shaded his limbs and torso. Bell shivered on brittle, stick-like legs, as the arm with the rubber band sought to steady the quaking frame against the wall. Bell mumbled something unintelligible, and he stumbled. Foster and Rivers managed to lunge to his side to catch him, before he tumbled to the floor. Foster let him lean against his large frame, as the other social worker led him back to his bed. Rivers glanced back at Foster, who nodded in understanding. Foster went out to the hallway to make the call.

Within minutes, Foster led two burly paramedics up the three flights to Bell's apartment. Foster handed out the psychiatric hold form, and Rivers secured the keys, which he would give to the landlord once he found him. Foster left the window open a crack, and then closed the locked door. "I don't think we'll have to worry about burglars," Foster said.

The social workers started back down the stairs, as Rivers shook his head. "Auschwitz," he sighed.

"Hmmm?" Foster asked.

"Haven't you seen those films…World War II…the concentration camps," Rivers explained. "When I saw him stand-ing in the hall, rail thin and quaking, thin, bald, my first thought was Auschwitz."

"Oh…yeah…" Foster muttered. "I know what you mean…Mr. Auschwitz."

"What a mess," Rivers said. "I'm telling you, these alcoholics will give up their food and their rent and their medical care…but the last thing they'll give up is that alcohol. And man, he was guzzling it down to the very end."

Chapter 11
NOVEMBER

"Come on in, Mr. Lofgren," Chuck Corley said as he led a corpulent, middle-aged man, in a gray suit and red tie, into the interview room closest to his office.

"Thanks for seeing me on such short notice, Chuck. I know you're a busy man." Lofgen said. "Call me Steve."

He picked a seat across from Corley at the interview room table. "I am the assistant to County Manager Ronald Morley. I've been on the phone with Jim Willis of Carlton & Madsen."

"Oh…this is about Mrs. Ogawa."

"You are familiar with the case, then," Lofgen stated rather tersely.

"Very much so," Corley answered, his hands folded in front of him on the table.

"And you have a social worker on the case?"

"Yes, we have an open case."

"I thought so. I was wondering – actually, Mr. Morley was wondering – why Mr. Willis keeps getting phone calls from an attorney from Cedarwood Paralegal Services named Etta Aguilar."

"Well," Corley said, "we decided it would be best to approach the case from this angle."

"Why is that?" Lofgen questioned, beads of perspiration beginning to gather on the top of his balding head.

"We decided it would be best to divide the work between our social worker and Ms. Aguilar. Our social worker would help Mrs. Ogawa find another home, while Ms. Aguilar – who has more experience in this these things – would communicate with the different entities involved in this case."

"But Aguilar does not work for the county. This case was referred to Adult Protective Services."

"Yes, well…" Corley explained quietly, "we decided it would be easier to keep loyalties clear and boundaries in tact this way."

"I see," Lofgen said, fidgeting in his chair. "I thought you were supposed to arrange for Mrs. Ogawa to go to the hospital."

Corley fixed his gaze on Lofgen, steeling himself to retain his composure. "Mr. Lofgen, a psychiatric hold is used when a person is a danger to herself or others. Mrs. Ogawa is a danger to no one. She is not holdable. She is a simple woman who has already been victimized by the system once in her life. She wants nothing more than to continue to live in this same simple manner. She is even willing to move, but she wants to be able to move to where she can continue to live the kind of life she's accustomed to. Unfortunately, this development is preventing her from doing that, and now we have a conflict."

"So," Lofgren said, "this woman is going to hold up a project that is liable to benefit an entire needy community?"

"Mrs. Ogawa does not want to hold up anything. She only wants to be compensated fairly for her loss. She is a simple woman, but not an unintelligent one. Her request seems rather reasonable to us."

"Reasonable?" Lofgen nearly shouted. "Is that what you call the demand Aguilar made on the city and the developer?"

"Yes, as a matter of fact," Corley nodded, "given the market value of her property, and the cost of real estate throughout the rest of the county, I would say this would be a very fair expectation."

"And to threaten to go to the press…to exploit this poor woman for the sake of publicity…to threaten to make the county, the city, and the entire project an object of public ridicule, because of a mistake President Roosevelt made fifty years ago?"

"A mistake…?" Corley said, shaking his head slightly. "First of all, as I explained, any contact with the media is being arranged through Ms. Aguilar.

"But you approve of it, don't you?"

"Whether I approve or disapprove of it is irrelevant," Corley said. "And as far as exploitation, I don't think it would do either of us any good to get into that debate. And as far as Roosevelt's "mistake" is concerned, do you have any idea what Mrs. Ogawa and other Japanese-Americans went through because of Executive Order 9033?"

"Well, I…," Lofgen coughed.

"Well, I do. I've studied it quite a lot. Mrs. Ogawa has endured enough for anyone's lifetime, believe me."

"Yes, well…"

"You know, Steve, we did not seek out this case. It was the developer who called us. It is our state-mandated responsibility to protect and advocate for vulnerable, elderly people in this county, and that is exactly what we are doing. We do not take what we do lightly; we do not use our authority haphazardly. The demands for Mrs. Ogawa are not unfair; our discussions are not unreasonable. As far as we're concerned, this is the least this woman deserves."

"Well," Lofgen sputtered, "you have made your position on this case very clear."

"I'm glad I could be clear, Steve."

"Mr. Morely will be very interested in all this. I'm certain this is not the last you will hear from the county manager."

"Tell him he's free to call," said Corley. "I'm here Monday through Friday, eight to five."

Donna Briar entered the Bullpen on a late Thursday morning, shaking her head and muttering, "Brrr…!"

"Cold again..?" Foster asked, peering over his shoulder at her.

"It's not just that," Briar whispered. She glanced about the cubicles to make sure no one else stood within ear-shot. "It's Sollie and Rhonda…"

Foster turned his chair and faced forward, his eyebrows peaked behind his bifocals. "Oh…?"

"Haven't you noticed?" Briar exclaimed.

"Noticed what…?" Foster returned.

"Remember three months ago…they were holding hands and gazing at each other like newlyweds. Now, they won't even talk to each other."

"Now that you mention it," Foster said. "I have noticed the silence over there, between their two desks."

'Yes," Briar said, "and in the unit meeting, Sollie came in late, and the only seat left was next to Rhonda. They didn't even look at each other, and everybody knew it…especially Chuck."

"Ooooops…" Foster shrugged.

"Yeah", Briar continued, "there's a lot of tension there. I don't know if Chuck's going to do anything about it, but it's getting pretty bad."

"Yeah," Foster said, "in all my years here, I've never known an office romance to last more than a few weeks. There are just too many things pulling in too many directions."

Suddenly Briar noticed Pagan heading toward the Bullpen. "Anyway…" Briar trailed off, as she headed quickly toward her cubicle. Foster picked up Briar's signal, and turned back to his desk. The nurse silently entered the Bullpen, her expression reduced to a fuming grimace. She glared quickly toward the two hot-line workers, almost daring them to comment. Then she snatched a form from the shelf, and marched back out of the Bullpen.

Briar and Foster exchanged glances, and shrugged their shoulders. "Oh, well…" Foster sighed.

The next day the tan county Oldsmobile sped down the freeway toward Meyersdale. Patrick Brennan shared the front seat with Sharon Roth, a pretty and bubbly, curly red-haired social worker from the county AIDS case management program. Roth asked Brennan to accompany her on a home visit, to determine whether a client's disability had progressed to the point of incapacity.

"So, how are things goin' over the hill in Henderson," Brennan asked. "Are you still workin' with horses, or ponies, or whatever…?"

"Yeah," said Roth, "we have a little riding stable, and we take kids out on the trail, help them get comfortable with the horse.

"Don't y' ride horses for show, too?" Brennan asked.

"I used to," nodded Roth, "but now my activities are restricted to the stable, and to recreational riding."

"My daughter, Lily, is beginning to make noises about ridin' a horse. What hours is your stable open?"

Usually on weekends, from 8:00 in the morning to about 6:00 in the evening," smiled Roth. "Give me a call and bring Lily by. We'd love to take her out on the trail. "Brennan paused a moment, and then changed the subject. "So, anyway...who are we seein' today?"

The effervescence immediately disappeared from Sharon Roth's demeanor, as her speech grew somber. "It's a very sad story," she said. "His name is Robert Hoffman. He's thirty-two years old. He had been a successful agent for an insurance company. He had been engaged, and he had lived with his fiancé in a nice apartment in Meyersdale. But he learned he had AIDS a year and a half ago. The disease spread rapidly, as he did not begin using the inhibitors as soon as he should. As his symptoms began to materialize, and his disease became widely known, his life slowly began to crumble.

"It turned out – unbeknownst to his fiancé – Robert had a homosexual affair three years ago, which is how he contracted the disease. But first because of denial, and then because of shame, he delayed getting tested. Once the fiancé found out, she left him. His only family – a brother in St. Louis – will not speak with him. His parents are dead. When his employer found out, Robert was laid off. They told him he would not be an effective or appropriate representative for the firm.

"I became involved about six months ago; the clinic where he was diagnosed referred him. Despite his diagnosis, he remained in denial for several more months, refusing treatment, and applying for no public assistance. When I got him, his T-cell count had already fallen to just below 200. He had grown weak and thin; he developed thrush in the mouth, and lesions on his legs and abdomen. Worst of all, he began growing demented, which made him increasingly difficult to work with as he grew more paranoid and volatile, as well as forgetful.

"I have never seen a client deteriorate so rapidly. If he had received help earlier, he probably would not be so sick now. He reminds me of the AIDS patients of the early 80's, when so little was known of the disease. In this day and age, he shouldn't be this sick, but he is. He is truly only a shadow of his prior self.

"I obtained SSI for him, and moved him into a low-income apartment. As he grew increasingly debilitated, we got in-home supportive services for him as well. But this morning I received a call from one of the workers, saying he had fired her, screamed at her, and chased her out with a broomstick, locking the door behind her. He's there now by himself. She says he's quite weak, and could easily fall and hurt himself.

"She didn't want to call 911?"

"The last thing Robert needs is a bunch of cops, paramedics, and firemen to come running around the place."

"Yeah," Brennan said. When you call 911, you get the whole package."

"I was hoping we could get to him first and talk to him, and see if we could bring him to the hospital a little more gently."

"I get it…"Brennan shrugged. "He lives in an apartment?"

"On the first floor," Roth said.

"Do you have a key…?"

"No, unfortunately…"

"What if the door's locked?" What if he doesn't let us in?"

"Well…I don't know," Sharon said. "The apartment is on the ground floor. We'll have to see what happens."

"Oh, bloody…" Brennan's voice trailed off.

Roth and Brennan reached Hoffman's apartment at about 11:30 am. The wind blew fiercely from the northwest. Hoffman's apartment complex stood against a busy thoroughfare which led from Meyersdale, in southern Cedarwood County, east to the next county. The complex had been targeted for renovation for many years, but the owner had yet to make the improvements. At night, the complex provided the backdrop for drug deals and prostitution; in the daylight, the poverty and neglect of the neighborhood could be readily discerned.

The social workers found Hoffman's apartment several doors away from the street. Roth knocked on the door, paused, and then knocked louder. "Hello…Robert? It's Sharon…Sharon Roth."

She and Brennan listened for movement within the apartment, perhaps footsteps making their way to the door. Nothing happened. "Uh-oh," she said.

She and Brennan peered into the window next to the door, and Brennan pushed against the window to determine if it would open. It would not.

"Shoot!" Roth exclaimed. "We need to get in there."

"We might have to call the police, Sharon. We can't just break in there."

"Shoot…wait, Patrick, there's a little patio at the back of the apartment. There's a sliding glass door. Let's go check it."

The social workers hurried around the corner of the building, past the scruffy planter boxes and patchy, dried lawn. They made their way to the six foot fence, which they both scaled with ease. Crossing the small patio, Roth pushed against the handle of the glass door, which slowly slid open. She parted the drapes from the door, and called inside.

"Robert?" Roth called again, a hint of anxiety touching her voice.

She and Brennan froze as they heard a moan from further inside the dwelling. They hastened to the bedroom at the end of the hall, and Roth gasped as she entered. "Oh…Robert..!"

In the corner of the bedroom, they found a man, laying in fetal position on the carpet beside his futon bed. He moaned and turned his head intermittently. A purple gash bloodied his forehead, indicating he had struck his head on the side table during a fall. A small puddle of urine formed around his hip and soaked into his underwear. A tiny puddle of pale, foamy saliva gathered between his dark cheek and the carpet. Hoffman's thin arms shivered as he held them around his torso. Roth could not tell if he was asleep or unconscious, but Brennan did not wait to find out. He immediately called for an ambulance.

Roth covered Hoffman with a blanket, deciding not to move him until the paramedics arrived. Every once in a while Hoffman would open his eyes, and attempt to make some sense of the circumstances, but then he would close his eyes and lay his head back down on the floor. At one point he looked up, apparently recognizing the auburn-haired social worker. "Sharon?" he whispered. "Is that you?"

She knelt beside him, placing her hand gently on his shoulder. "It's me, Robert."

"Where am I?" he begged.

"You're on the floor of your bedroom," Roth said. "Did you fall out of bed?"

"I don't know," Hoffman moaned. "I don't remember. What happened? Where is everybody?" he pleaded, tears rolling down his cheek. "Where did everybody go?"

"Take it easy, Robert," Roth answered, fighting to control her own tears as Hoffman lowered his head back down upon the floor. Brennan handed Roth a pillow from the bed, which she gently placed under Hoffman's head. He lapsed back into sleep.

"He looks terrible," Roth gasped, "much worse than I've ever seen him. He's deteriorated so fast – much faster than anyone else I've known. He seems to be breathing okay, but he looks feverish. God, Patrick, this is terrible!"

Within a few moments the paramedics arrived. They gently lifted Hoffman from the floor and placed him on his back on the gurney. They rolled him out the front door toward the ambulance, parked out on the curb. Sharon Roth made certain she took Hoffman's keys, and she locked the apartment – including the sliding glass door – before she and Brennan left.

Roth sat quietly on the ride back. She leaned her forehead onto her finger tips, which she used to massage her aching brown. Brennan allowed her to sit quietly for a bit, and then gently broke the silence.

"So, what happens now?" he asked.

"I guess I'll refer the case for conservatorship," Roth signaled. "His condition is not going to improve. He'll probably have to be placed in the residential care home in Baldwyn."

"Geez…"

"You know, Patrick," she said. "It's not the disease that's killing Robert Hoffman. It's his world's reaction to the disease: his whole world abandoned him when they found out he had AIDS, when they found out he had sex with another man. He didn't change that much, but his entire life – all his loved ones, everything he had counted on – turned on him, and left him by himself. I know that's what's killing him; if he still had the support, the disease could be managed much more easily.

Brennan placed his free hand on her shoulder. "What are y' gonna do?"

"I don't know", Roth shook her head. "It's just so sad."

The county car squeezed inside one of the parking spaces to the west of the Health Department Building. Brennan switched off the ignition, and he and Roth sat silently in the car for a moment.

"You see a lot of death in your work, don't you Sharon?"

"Yeah," she answered, wiping an eye with the back of her hand, "not as much as I used to, but still…you'd think I'd be used to this by now. But this one…this one happened too fast. I normally have time to prepare both myself and the client, but not this time…"

Roth pulled out a handkerchief and dabbed her eyes. The two social workers sat silently again, until she said, "You were a priest once, weren't you Patrick?"

"Well, I studied at the seminary for a while…"

"What happened?"

Brennan paused momentarily, and then said, "You mean, why didn't I become a priest?"

She nodded.

"Well, let's just say the church and I had a few irreconcilable differences."

"Do you still believe in God…in heaven?" asked Roth.

"Well, not like the church teaches – that was once of the irreconcilable differences – but I suppose I believe in a version of God…not so well defined, you know…"

"What about heaven?"

"I don't know," Brennan said. "I don't know what will happen after I die…?"

"I was raised Presbyterian," Roth said, "but I haven't really been to church or prayed in a long time. It's awfully hard to believe in a God that let's people suffer they way they do."

"I know what y' mean," Brennan agreed. "And it's hard t' believe in a God that would let people suffer simply t' allow people like us t' to charitable works, or t' learn some kind of lesson. It seems a bit ridiculous.

"Yeah…it's hard to figure out."

"I remember one woman," Brennan said. "She had dementia, and she could barely walk, and the landlord was ready t' evict her because she couldn't keep track of paying the rent. She began wanderin' the halls of the apartment building, and she would fall, until the fire department called us repeatedly to do somethin' about it. She had no family, no one who could act on her behalf. Finally, I was called out to place her on a hold, and she eventually was conserved.

"I remember her just before the paramedics strapped her into the gurney. She reached into a drawer and pulled out a medal…y' know, the kind you hang on the rear view mirror of your car. The medal featured an engravin' of an angel, and I distinctly remember the words:

Protect me, my passengers, and all who I pass by
with a steady hand and a watchful eye.

"I'll never forget it. Here was this poor woman, unable t' walk, or even take care of herself. And yet she gave me this Guardian Angel t' protect me in my car. Hell, she hadn't driven in years…but she believed so much in angels, she wanted to share one with me. I figured hell, if this poor wretch of a woman could have hope, I guess I could too. And what the hell is God anyway, but the embodiment of hope."

Sharon Roth leaned across the car seat toward Patrick Brennan, placing her arms around his neck. "Sometimes it's so easy to forget why I became a social worker," she sniffed, crying softly.

"Oh, bloody hell…" Brennan said, "…I forgot a long time ago."

Despite Steve Lofgen's threats, Chuck Corley never heard from the county manager's office. Instead, on the following Tuesday, Ari Davis drove the Oldsmobile, through the town of Maple Creek, with Jane Ogawa sitting in the back seat as a passenger. She had tied her grayish black hair into a bun, which outlined her pleasant face and her steel-rimmed glasses. Ogawa wore a simple flowered dress, and sat quietly watching the scenery pass by. Her small but sturdy hands - toughened by years of gardening – lay folded in her lap as they passed through this new, unfamiliar city. She told Davis she had only been out of Rogers Park a handful of times in the past forty years, and remained quite unfamiliar with the other towns in the county.

"So, how long will you be helping me, Ms. Davis," she called.

"Just until you get settled into your new home, and the negotiations with the city and the developer are complete," Davis said. "The judge thought it would be best if we represented you during the complicated process."

"I appreciate it, Ms. Davis," Ogawa said. "I have no desire to meet with lawyers and agents. I just want my garden. That is what is important to me."

"I know, Mrs. Ogawa," Davis said. "This will be all over soon."

Davis parked the car in front of a stucco, single-level home. A green carpet-like law surrounded by a garden of emerald shrubs and bright flowers spread out before the house.

Mrs. Ogawa squinted through her glasses and she studied the structure. "It looks very nice," she said, "...looks a little like my home."

"Yes, and there's a market and a bank within a couple of blocks of here," Davis said. "Come on, let's take a look."

Davis rolled out of the driver's seat, and went around to help Mrs. Ogawa out the passenger door. "Can we look at the back yard first?"

"Of course we can, honey," Davis said. "I know how important your garden is to you. I think you'll like this."

The Deputy Public Guardian and the woman walked around through the side gate to the back yard. They walked along a tiny cement patio which led to an extensive redwood deck, surrounded by young fruit trees. Budding rose bushes lightly touched the fringe of the deck.

On either side of the deck extended two patches of freshly overturned earth: one 150 square feet, the other less than one hundred. A hose stretched from a spigot onto the closest patch, and a collection of tools – a hoe, a rake, a trowel, and a shovel – leaned against the north end of the redwood fence surrounding the property. Mrs. Ogawa stooped down to scoop a handful of earth, which he sifted expertly through her fingers. She held it up to her nose to smell. "Very nice…" she said. "I can transplant my vegetables and herbs here."

"That's what we thought," Davis smiled.

Ari Davis showed her the inside of the house as well, but Ogawa considered it irrelevant: the garden convinced her. Although reluctant to move from her beloved home for forty years, this appeared to be the best alternative.

As they returned to the county car, Mrs. Ogawa turned to Ari Davis, bowing slightly, and said, "Thank you, Ms. Davis, for your kindness – you, Mr. Rivers, and Ms. Aguilar. You have all been very kind."

"Not at all," Davis said. "That's why we're here."

A temporary conservatorship had been granted to the public guardian over Mrs. Ogawa, as the judge felt her "cultural challenge" would prevent her from advocating in her best interest.

Although the conservatorship could have been dropped once the sale of the house was finished, Mrs. Ogawa seemed to appreciate not having to manage her finances any more. The conservatorship became permanent, allowing Ogawa to concentrate only on the gardening she loved so dearly.

Several days later, Sollie Rivers wandered into his supervisor's office. "You wanted to see me, Chuck?"

"Yes, Sollie," Corley said. "I want you and Rhonda to go out and see a woman in Fayette. It sounds like she has some health problems as well as case management issues."

"Can't Patrick or Bob go?" Rivers asked.

"No, I think it's important you and Rhonda go. It will be a good opportunity."

Rivers studied his boss' expression for a moment, immediately understanding the direction to which Corley was headed. "Rhonda knows already. You shouldn't waste any more time. Why don't you guys go and take care of it now."

Rivers sighed. "Okay, Chuck, you're right."

Sollie Rivers and Rhonda Pagan sat in silence as Rivers drove the Tempo five miles east toward the woman's house. Rivers steered the car onto the appropriate street, but parked several houses before the client's home. As he switched off the ignition, both he and Pagan suddenly spoke. "We have to talk," they both said.

Rivers smiled at Pagan, as they both turned to face each other in the front seat. "This is ridiculous, Ronnie," Rivers said. "We shouldn't be treating each other like this."

"I know, Sollie," Pagan said. "We are two very different people, and we just don't make a really good couple. What we shared was very nice, and very refreshing for me, but I think we've taken it as far as it can go."

"I agree," Rivers said. "And, by the way, I'm sorry for the other day. I shouldn't have gotten so excited."

"Well, gosh Sollie," Pagan smiled, "you never get excited."

"Yeah," grinned Rivers, "I'm such a stoic."

"I'm sorry, too," said Pagan. "I don't know why I would expect you to change in a few days manners and habits you've been working on your whole life. I think we are just spending too much time with each other – at work and at each other's home. Actually, I think I've had it with relationships for a while. I think I need a little time off."

"I agree..." Rivers said, "...although I have enjoyed some of our time together..."

"Me, too…" Pagan smiled enticingly. The two embraced, and kissed each other tenderly.

They paused to sigh, and then Rivers said, "Well, let's go see this woman."

"I've got a feeling there won't be much for us to do," said Pagan.

"Yeah," said Rivers, "I think this is the reason Church wanted us to go on a home visit together. I think we've been letting our personal lives spill onto the work place, and I think he wanted us to clear it up."

"Not bad for a boss, huh?" nodded Pagan.

"We're pretty lucky," said Rivers. "C'mon, Ronnie, let's go."

The next day Rivers received word that Mr. Auschwitz – Edgar Bell – had died three days after he and Foster brought him to the hospital. The cirrhosis of the liver – leaking toxics from his liver into his body – combined with his continuous bouts of malnutrition and dehydration, proved simply too much for his weak, ravaged body. He died in his sleep, alone in a hospital room on a Thursday afternoon. Because no one – not even the original anonymous referent – came forward to claim the body, no burial provision had been made for Mr. Bell. The hospital turned Bell's body over to the coroner, to dispose of the remains.

Rivers received another phone call, one which would turn around his day for the positive.

"Good morning, Sollie Rivers," he answered his phone.

"Mr. Rivers?" a gentle male voice spoke over the line.

"Yes?" Rivers answered, trying to recognize the voice.

"It's Edward," the voice answered.

"Edward…?" Rivers said. "Edward Nichols?"

"Yes…" Nichols said.

It's good to hear your voice, Edward," Rivers exclaimed. "How are you? For that matter, where are you?"

"I was discharged from the hospital about a week ago. I'm selling our house, and I've moved into an assisted living community in

Meyersdale. I've met a lot of new people there. It's really quite exciting."

"So it's working out for you?"

"Yes, I had a chance to think about it while I was in the hospital, and I decided it would be a good move for me...gives me a chance to meet other people...get on with my life..."

"How long were you in the hospital?" Rivers asked.

"Oh, about six weeks...it was touch and go there for a while, but I think I'm over the worst. I am taking my medications this time, and I see a psychiatrist on a regular basis."

"Good, good..." Rivers said, "...because you know, Edward, even though the grief may lessen, it never totally goes away. It will probably resurface from time to time, especially for a couple as close as you and Mary..."

"That's what they tell me..." Nichols said. "I know now I was slowly killing myself while Mary was dying. But I was mostly afraid of being alone. I know now I don't have to be alone, and I realize Mary would want me to live on...to enjoy life..."

"That's great, Edward," Rivers cheered.

"Anyway, Sollie, I just wanted to take a moment to thank you. I know if it weren't for you, I wouldn't be alive right now. You saved my life, and I am very grateful."

"It was my pleasure, Edward," Rivers said. "You're a good man, and I'm glad things are working out for you."

"Thank you, Sollie. God bless you."

"You're welcome, Edward," Rivers said, "take care."

Rivers hung up the phone with a satisfied sigh, and felt that old familiar warm sensation inside.

When he mentioned to Brennan that Nichols had called, and what he had said, Brennan nodded. "Oh, yeah, Sharon and I were tryin' to remember why we became social workers."

"Yeah, well every once in a while," Rivers said, "I get to remember."

Chapter 12
DECEMBER

The one hundred and thirty three staff persons of Adult Services gathered in the multipurpose room of the Health Department building. The first Tuesday of every other month featured the All Staff meeting in its schedule. "All Staff" usually entailed an address by Adult Services Director Marlene Gregg, on some pertinent or semi-pertinent, division wide issue, or perhaps a training or lecture on some topic of county government concern. The meetings normally rated among Adult Services staff from mildly intriguing to downright boring. On this particular Tuesday, however, a special presentation had been planned.

Not normally a readily personable individual, Marlene Gregg did not particularly relish the chance to interact with her underlings, but she felt such an appearance now and again to be important for division spirit. Forceful and often gruff in small interpersonal interactions, Gregg normally left such morale-building exercises to her deputy administrators. Although some staff seemed to quake in her intimidating presence, everyone respected her for the prestige she brought to the division, and for the ferocity with which she advocated for her program.

The APS staff gathered in the far corner of the noisy room, giggling, among themselves as they nibbled on bagels and donuts from the buffet line arranged for the meeting. Bob Foster and Sollie Rivers debated the collective fate of the local basketball team, while Rhonda Pagan and Emma Hayes discussed stories from graduate school. Chuck Corley ardently encouraged all to attend this particular meeting, intimating something special involving them would take place.

Suddenly, the far door swung open, and Marlene Gregg strode into the room with her usual commanding, get-it-done gait. She wore a dark brown pantsuit emphasizing her tall, authoritative form. Following Gregg stepped a short, thin, nerdish man with curly brown hair and gold-framed glasses. The man wore a stiff blue business suit, and clasped a manila envelope under his arm.

As the staff sat forward in rows of blue plastic chairs, Gregg cleared her throat and spoke toward the assemblage.

"Before we commence with announcements and other business, we have a special presentation. For those who don't know, this is Supervisor Reuben Madsen. He is here to present a special commendation to the APS unit."

"Thank you, Marlene," the supervisor said. "I am happy to be here, to offer special recognition to a very special team. Four years ago, when Marlene Gregg developed this new model of Adult Services Intake, there were many on the board and in the county manager's office that were skeptical. Marlene proposed to spend money and use staff for Adult Services in ways no other county had ever attempted. Most other counties were satisfied with responding to only the most serious APS cases, spending no time in preventing serious situations before they arose. Many of us felt Marlene's proposal would not be cost effective. Now, we see the error of our judgments. Marlene convinced us that – because Cedarwood County consisted of such a substantial population of adults over sixty-five, and disabled adults – this system would be the most effective use of the taxpayer's money. She proved to be right.

"By loading the APS unit with veteran professionals with superior knowledge of the county and its residents, the Adult Protective Services unit now serves as a model for the rest of the state, as well as much of the country. The inordinate number of letters and phone calls we get from professionals, law enforcement agencies, the medical community, and the grateful public, praising the work of APS seems to bear this out. This unit makes Marlene – and all of county government – look very, very good.

"Therefore, in recognition of the unit's outstanding work and service in assisting and protecting the vulnerable adult population of Cedarwood County, I read to you the following proclamation composed in part by APS supervisor Chuck Corley:

"The primary duties of Cedarwood County Adult Protective Services include: The Hotline, Adult Protective Services, Probate Conservatorship Investigation, Senior Liaison, 24-hour response, short-term case management, and adult abuse reporting training in the community.

"You are a dedicated, committed, highly-skilled and professional staff. You are very supportive to each other and maintain a good sense of humor and positive outlook.

With much determination and compassion, you tackle some of the more complicated and urgent human problems to pass through Adult Services.

"You are asked to assess your client's capacity, rule out undue influence, consider the least restrictive intervention, and respect their right to self-determination.

One of the more challenging aspects of your work is to advocate for your client's best interest, and you have a strong commitment to do so. This often means educating an anxious community that voices demand that you 'do something'.

"Over the past few years it has been exciting to witness Adult Protective Services evolve from a multi-disciplinary unit to a dynamic multi-disciplinary team. Your willingness to trust, risk, voice your concern and opinions has nurtured a sage environment in which to debate the infinite complex issues that confront you everyday in your work. Your comfort level to raise and challenge "business as usual" concerning the operation of the unit has been instrumental in its present and continued evolution.

"Your creativity and innovation are encouraged and welcomed as this agency moves forward with change, to better meet the needs of the growing dependent and frail population of Cedarwood County.

"Therefore, in recognition of your outstanding service to the County of Cedarwood, the Board of Supervisors commends the Adult Protective Services Unit, also known as the "Do Something Crew".

The whole of Adult Services staff clapped and hooted as Supervisor Madsen urged the Adult Protective Services staff to stand. The seven APS workers grinned and blushed, until the applause eventually died down. Finally, Marlene Gregg motioned them to sit down, as she addressed the unit herself.

"I, as well, viewed the reformation of Adult Protective Services with some trepidation," Gregg said. "But Chuck kept assuring me it would work out and, obviously, he was right. And now, finally, the vision of a pro-active unit, which addressed problems before they became crises, had come to fruition in you seven extraordinary workers.

"You are the cutting edge in this county, between sustainability and poverty; between independence and institutionalization; between health and illness; between safety and risk; between life and death, in so many ways. You are the front line, the safety net, for the people in this county who are otherwise ignored, devalued, disenfranchised, and debilitated. By dealing with the people no one else wants to deal with, you not only help those individuals, but you help society maintain its overall stability.

"But this line cannot hold forever. Someday, this society is going to have to reckon with the ills that befall its disadvantaged factions. It is going to have to learn to take better care of its weaker links, or someday the chain will invariably rust and collapse. Until then, I commend your courage, your initiative, and your compassion.

Through the lengthy proceedings, Sollie Rivers sat rather impatiently, fidgeting like a school boy awaiting recess. But as soon as Gregg closed the meeting, he glanced over at Ari Davis and said, "You ready?"

"Yes I am…" Davis said. "Patrick?"

Brennan nodded, and the three rose from their chairs in unison. Brennan had already reserved the Oldsmobile. After the three gathered up the various documentation and equipment they would need, the loaded into the county care: Rivers and Davis in the front, and Brennan in the back. They headed to Huntington to issue a 3701 form.

Patrick Brennan had received an anonymous call two weeks previous concerning an elderly woman named Mildred Messanich, who lived by herself in a large estate in the upper hills of Huntington. The caller, who claimed to be a neighbor but refused to give her name, said she felt Messanich needed some help managing her money, and could be vulnerable to undue influence. At eighty-nine years, Messanich may have been worth more that three million dollars. Typically dressed in a flowered dress, her hair fixed in a bun, Messanich suffered from dementia. She presented with poor memory, frequent disorientation, and the inability to devise and follow through with plans. The neighbor reported to have seen cash around the house, and had noticed unpaid utility and telephone bills. The caller had reported a strange man who had been coming around the house, for a purpose unknown to the referent. The referent said Messanich had no relatives in the area, and feared the strange man might be interested in taking advantage of the older woman.

Given the amount of money concerned, and given the age and apparently cognitive capacity of Mildred, Brennan decided to open a case. Chuck assigned it to Rivers.

Rivers had made a home visit to the Messanich estate the previous Friday. He conducted an informal mini-mental status exam, and determined the Mildred was indeed showing signs of dementia, and was in need of protection. When he asked her about how she pays her bills, she hesitated and mumbled a bit, and after considerable searching, showed him her checkbook. Rivers found dozens of check stubs written to a local market, which appeared to be in the handwriting of someone other than Mildred. Many checks had been written to "Cash" also in another's handwriting. Rivers also found check stubs written to utility companies, the telephone company, and other collectors – again in someone else's script. These entries seemed to go back many months.

"Who has been helping you with these bills?" Rivers asked.

"The police officer," Mildred answered directly. "He's such a nice man, so kind to offer to run so many errands for me. He goes to the store, and to the bank, anywhere I want, to buy something or to exchange money. I barely need to leave the house at all, or worry about paying bills."

"Who is this police officer?"

"His name is Kurt...Kurt...um, let's see...Kurt Shrader, that's it."

"Kurt Shrader...does he work for the Huntington Police Department?"

"Oh, yes...I feel so safe with him around," she said.

"I can understand that," Rivers said, as he mulled the situation over in his mind. "How long has he been helping you like this?"

"Um...let's see...a long time, ever since my Matty died."

"Your Matty...?"

"Yes, my brother," she said. "Matty lived with me here until he passed away."

"And Officer Shrader has helped you ever since?"

"Yes...I don't know what I would have done without him."

"Does Officer Shrader visit you in uniform?" Rivers asked.

"Sometimes..." she answered, "...and sometimes not. He visits on weekends, and at night sometimes."

"That's very nice of him," Rivers said, his eyes growing wide with the gravity of what Mildred's statements were suggesting. It became clear early to Rivers that he was holding the short fuse to a powder keg. The trick for Rivers would be to find out the exact nature of the situation without lighting the fuse too soon.

"Does Officer Shrader cook and clean for you too?"

"No, I have a girl come in for that. Betty...no, Mamie...she comes during the day to fix my meals, and to help me clean a little."

"Where's Mamie today?" Rivers asked.

"She's not here? Oh, yes...today is her day off."

"Do you have enough help in the home with her?"

"Oh, sure, I don't need much help."

"Is it ever difficult to manage here by yourself? This is an awfully big house for only one person."

"Where else would I go...?"

There are probably some nice communities you could afford, where there would be plenty of people around to help you."

Oh, no," Mildred said. "I don't what to move to an old folk's home. This is my home, and this is where I want to live the rest of my life."

"I see," Rivers nodded.

"Besides, I can get along fine without help."

"Except for Kurt Shrader, right?"

"Who..?"

"You know...Officer Shrader, the nice policeman who runs errands for you."

"Oh, yes...Kurt Shrader. You know, he goes to the grocery store, and to the bank for me."

"That is very nice of him."

Rivers asked if he could take a look around the house, just to see its current state. The entire house appeared very neat and tidy, but a substantial layer of dust coated most of the rooms – evidence of their lack of use. The ranch style house seemed to spread out forever, and Rivers counted seven rooms aside from Mildred's living room, kitchen, and bedroom, the rooms she utilized most.

As Rivers ventured further into the back rooms of the house, he found one particular bedroom which seemed more lived in than the others. The furniture seemed much more modern than in the others, and pencils and notepaper rested on the dresser, indicating someone had been in the room recently. Rivers walked through the bedroom and the adjacent bathroom, where a door opened to reveal a tile floor leading to a glass shower stall door. To his astonishment, the social worker found two large and worn shopping bags on the floor of the shower stall. Looking inside, he found both bags to be filled with money.

"Oh, my God," Rivers said, as he peered into the second sack. Both bags contained stacks of ten and twenty dollar bills. "There must be $50,000 here." He placed the bags carefully on the floor, and considered for a moment what he had witnessed. "Ari Davis," he mumbled to himself.

Though not his favorite person in the world, he knew she excelled at her job. She could act quickly and decisively to protect

Mildred's money. He walked back to the front room, to broach to Mildred his discovery.

"So, do you keep cash around the house?" Rivers asked, once he settled back in the front room.

Mildred looked quizzically at the social worker, and asked "What do you mean?"

Rivers waited a moment, and then asked, "I mean, you don't keep loose cash around the house, do you?"

"Heaven's no," Mildred said, "that wouldn't be safe. Any cash I have I give to Officer Shrader, who puts it in the bank for me."

"It must be reassuring to have a police officer available so much."

"Oh, yes, I don't know what I'd do without him."

"Are you able to dress and shower by yourself?" Rivers asked.

"I can dress myself okay, but it's too hard to get in and out of the shower or bath. Mamie will give me a sponge bath now and again. Otherwise, I haven't used a tub or a shower in a long time."

Rivers left Mildred's house very nervous, sensing an impending crisis. When he reached the Adult Services office, he immediately approached Ari Davis' cubicle, and explained the situation. As he predicted, Davis acted immediately, saying she and Rivers should return to the Messanich home and take possession of the money. It should be deposited in her bank account, where it will be safe, she said.

Taking the case to Corley, all three agreed upon the unusual circumstances by which the police officer became involved with a client – even in Huntington. A clear conflict of interest, it seems Mildred Messanich completely trusted Officer Shrader, making her the perfect candidate for financial abuse and undue influence. They agreed Rivers and Davis would come out to the Messanich house on Thursday, and they should bring Brennan to help collect and count the money in the shower stall.

Corley told Rivers, for political correctness sake, it would probably be a good idea to get a statement from the officer. Strictly speaking, said Corley, they did not know if the officer had actually done anything illegal; unethical, perhaps; inappropriate, certainly, but at the moment, they could see nothing illegal. Serious allegations seemed to be developing, said Corley, and Rivers should at least hear what the officer says before going any further. Rivers argued with Corley saying warning the officer could place the woman's money in jeopardy, but Corley insisted Rivers call the officer directly.

He never got the chance. When Rivers returned to his own cubicle, he found a message on his voice mail from Kurt Shrader. Rivers took a deep breath to calm himself, and called back the officer.

Kurt Shrader answered in a deep, serious voice, which seemed to emphasize the toughness of the man. River detected a note of restraint in the voice, as effort to remain calm which occasionally betrayed a hint of anxiety. Rivers introduced himself, and told him the nature of the referral concerning Mildred Messanich.

"Who made the referral?" Shrader queried.

"We don't know," replied Rivers. "It came to us anonymously."

"And you decided to take it seriously?"

"Well, given her age, and the amount of money we're talking about, we decided to look into it."

"And the referent told you about me?" said Shrader.

"Well, the referent said something about a man who comes around the house. Mrs. Messanich was the one who gave me your name."

"Yeah, she mentioned you had come by the house, and she showed me your card," Shrader said. "That's why I called. So what's going to happen now?"

"Well, we're trying to determine whether she's going to need some help or not, or even if she needs a conservator. She's pretty forgetful, and it sounds like she has some trouble keeping track of her money."

"You don't think I can safeguard her money for her?" Shrader asked pointedly.

Rivers did not like the tone of that question.

"Well, Officer, obviously you can't be there all the time. She seems to have some trouble paying her bills, and she certainly would be a target for undue influence."

"I get it," he replied, more than a lilt of impatience in his voice.

"So, how long have you known Mrs. Messanich?" Rivers asked.

"Oh, a long time," Shrader said.

"She said you've been helping her ever since her brother died."

"Yeah, I have," Shrader said. "Is there anything wrong with that?"

"Not necessarily," Rivers said, drawing on his considerable diplomatic skills, "but again, you can't be watching over her twenty-four hours a day, given your duties with the police department. I can imagine someone like Mildred would take up a lot of your time, if she could."

"Well, Mr. Rivers, I think that's something for me to worry about, don't you?"

"Of course," Rivers responded. "We just want to make sure she has all the care and protection she needs."

"I get it," Shrader said. "Are you planning to visit her again?"

"Probably, as the investigation goes on."

"When you are going out there again, I'd like to be there as well."

"I'm not sure," Rivers said, deciding to play his cards close to his chest."

"Could you let me know?" the officer requested. "I'd like to be there next time."

"Can I ask why?"

The officer's anger seemed to intensify. "Because I feel as if Millie needs some support, before you come back out and grill her again…"

"I'm not going to grill…"

"She's an old woman, and she's not used to strangers. I don't want to see her conserved, and her home and property taken away, if she doesn't need it. Sometimes she can get confused. I want to be there for her, to help her deal with this."

"Well again, Officer Shrader," River spoke calmly, "I'm not sure what we'll be doing next. Can I get back you about this?"

Shrader sort of snorted, and then calmed himself, trying to return the conversation to a congenial tone. "I would appreciate it if you would."

"Oh, sure," Rivers said, "I'll get back to you."

Rivers exhaled deeply as he hung up the phone. "Phew!" he said.

Rivers immediately consulted with Corley, telling him about his conversation. "It sounds like he's getting nervous," Corley suggested.

"Yeah," said Rivers, "I decided not to give him the date of our visit because I get a sense he could go a little nuts on us. I mean, I'm not quite sure what he's doing, but now I'm convinced he's doing something he shouldn't be."

"You already knew that," Corley counseled. "As a uniformed police officer, it's highly inappropriate to be providing personal favors to residents, and certainly not help them manage their money."

"Do you think we should get back over to the house sooner than Thursday?"

"No, if the money disappears – after everything Mrs. Messanich told you – Shrader will be in even more trouble. Just go out on Thursday as you planned, and we'll go from there."

On Monday, Corley took a call from Devin Fitgerald, Chief of Police for Huntington. Fitzgerald explained how Kurt Shrader had come into his officer yesterday, and told him about how he's been helping Mrs. Messanich., and how now there is a report to Adult Protective Services.

"You have to understand, Chuck," Fitzgerald said, "Huntington is a unique town. There is, therefore, a greater expectation about how much a police officer might do for a resident."

"So, what Officer Shrader is doing with Mrs. Messanich is considered standard procedure in Huntington?"

"Well, I have to admit his involvement with Mrs. Messanich is a little too much," the Chief conceded, "and believe me, I've warned him about this. So, I don't think you'll have to worry about Mrs. Messanich."

"Good," Corley said. "I mean, just the questions that arise in the community, when it looks as if a police officer might be taking advantage of a rich old woman."

"I agree," said Fitzgerald. Look, Chuck…it is Chuck, isn't it?"

"Chuck is fine."

"Look, can you do me a favor?"

Corley hesitated for a moment, and then asked, "What is it?"

"When your worker goes out to see Mrs. Messanich, Kurt would really like to be there as well. He feels she can be easily upset, and feels his presence would be good for everyone in the situation. He thinks he can help you do your job, and put your fears to rest."

"Well, Chief, I'll have to check with my case worker about when he's going out again. I'll have to get back you about that."

"That would be great," he said. "I sure would appreciate it." Fitzgerald said, sounding a lot like Shrader.

"Okay, I'll call you back," Corley said, clicking the phone off.

Corley stepped out of his office and called Rivers to him. "I just spoke to Chief Fitzgerald, of the Huntington Police Department."

"What the hell is going on, Chuck?" Rivers said.

"I think the Chief is a little embarrassed by all this," Corley said calmly. "I think the extra attention paid by Shrader toward Mrs. Messanich is probably fairly common practice in Huntington, except now Shrader's hand has been caught a little too far inside the cookie jar. I think Fitzgerald is trying to save face, and he's giving Shrader a chance to save face as well. I think he wants to protect his officer, but at the same time he does not want what goes on in Huntington to become common public knowledge."

"So what does he want?" Rivers asked.

"He wants me to let him know when you're going out again, so Officer Shrader can join you."

"What?"

"Fitzgerald says Shrader thinks he can be of help to you, to make Mrs. Messanich feel more comfortable."

"She was perfectly comfortable yesterday. I don't need his help."

"I know, Sollie," said Corley, "but for political sake, I think we need to let the officer – and the department – save face."

"Yeah, well I don't trust him," Rivers said.

"I know," Corley returned. "I'm going to accommodate the Chief, but I'm going to ask him to have another officer accompany Shrader on the home visit, just in case. It might help keep a lid on whatever might happen at the Messanich house."

"Okay," Rivers said, "I guess we have to be politically correct. I would feel better if Shrader didn't even know we went out. I hope the other cop is honest, at least."

"Well, take Ari and Patrick with you. Go ahead and place the cash in the bank, and freeze all the accounts. If he tries to stop you, there will be three of you plus the other officer as witnesses. That should be enough of a deterrent."

"I hope so," Rivers sighed.

So, after the All-Staff meeting – with Sollie Rivers driving, Ari Davis beside him and Patrick Brennan in the back – the gold county Oldsmobile winded it way through the serpentine streets of Huntington. The social workers gasped and giggled as they passed the huge estates of this prosperous hamlet. They watched long driveways reach back to opulently grand mansions, with groves of eucalyptus trees shading rich green lawns among tennis courts, swimming pools, and multi-car garages. Rolls Royce, Jaguar, Mercedes-Benz, BMW – these were the cars that filled those garages. Migrant gardeners wandered about the grounds, motorized leaf blowers growling, as they cleared the lawns and pathways of unwanted debris.

Block after block, these modern castles rolled past, very much reminding the APS workers of their own niches in the economic tapestry. Their mouths gaped – as they did every time they passed through this town – as they witnessed the incredible, luxuriant wealth and unsurpassed power accumulated among the elite of the county. Much of this old money had begun developing before the turn of the century, was now invested in the very fabric of the regional economics, providing the basis for much of the abundance of the area. The county workers giggled because they know on their government salaries this is a neighborhood they are never likely to call their own.

The Oldsmobile stopped in front of the Messanich manor. The ranch-styled home, surrounded by a green iron fence with a gate situated at the driveway, stretched out over the acreage which reached up the hill.

"Well, here we are," Rivers said. "Where are the officers?"

"I don't know." Davis said. "I say we give them about five minutes, and then we go in ourselves. Is Mamie here today?"

"She should be," Rivers said, "it's Tuesday."

"She can let us in," Davis said.

"Damn, I feel like we're on a dragnet or something," Rivers giggled nervously.

"I hope this guy doesn't lose it."

"Y' think he will?" Brennan asked.

"Who know?" Rivers said. "He seemed pretty stressed out. Hopefully, the other officer that comes with him will keep him calm, but I don't trust this police department."

"Have you ever been to the police station?" Brennan asked.

"No," Rivers said, "pretty wild?"

"It's like a bloody country club, Sollie," Brennan said. "Huntington isn't like anywhere else. I'll bet there's conflicts of interest we couldn't even imagine."

"Well, I…"

"Wait…look…" Davis pointed, "…who's that?"

A gray Jeep Wrangler pulled up to the driveway. A tall, silver-haired man with a mustache – probably in his forties – stepped out of the driver's side. "That's Kurt Shrader, I'll bet," Rivers said. The man, dressed in jeans and a gold shirt, turned a key inside he electronic gate release, and watched the iron fence roll back. The Wrangler then rolled into the driveway. Out of the vehicle stepped a red-haired man, similar in height to Shrader, dressed in a police-man's uniform.

"Shit, where's the police unit?" Rivers stammered.

Brennan read his mind. "This officer came in Shrader's car? What if he bloody tries t' run for it? What's the cop going to do, chase him on foot?"

"This is real stupid!" Rivers said. "It feels like a set up to me."

"Well, come on," Davis said, in her typical bull-dog style, "at least we have a car. Let's go get this money."

"Are we going to count the money here?" Brennan asked.

"I don't think so," said Rivers.

"Yes,", said Davis, I think we should just get the money, and then they can count it at the bank. We should spend as little time here as possible."

"Let's go," Rivers said.

"Cheap thrills…" Brennan grumbled, "…paid vacation."

As Davis, Rivers, and Brennan approached the gate, Shrader immediately crossed the driveway to intercept their path. He stood directly in front of the driveway, as if impeding the social workers' ability to enter."

"Good morning," Davis said, "I'm Arielle Davis from the Public Guardian's office. This is Sollie Rivers, and Patrick Brennan."

"This is Pete Newell," Shrader said, pointing to the red-haired uniformed officer.

"Ma'am," the officer responded. Newell wore a pained expression on his face, as if he knew he stood in the middle of a battle-field, with both sides aiming their weapons.

"So, why is the Public Guardian here?" Shrader asked, standing uneasily with hand hands on his hips, still blocking the gate.

"I've got a court order to take possession of the cash in Midred Messanich's house, to deposit it in the bank, and to freeze the accounts pending a conservatorship investigation."

"What?" Shrader bristled, almost shouting. He pointed his index finger at Davis. "You have no right…this is Mildred's money."

"Can I see the order?" Officer Newell asked. Davis handed him the document. "It looks like it's in order, Kurt," he said, placing a steadying hand on his colleague's shoulder. "You better let them do their job. We can sort all this out later."

"Shit, Pete," Shrader growled, shuffling out of the way as Davis and Brennan passed. The three APS workers entered the house, followed by Shrader and Newell. Mamie came to the door-way, followed by Mildred Messanich.

"What's going on here?" Mildred called. "Kurt...Kurt, what are these people doing here?"

"They're from the county, Millie," Shrader told her. "They're here to put the money in the bank".

"What money?" Mildred said, flustered and confused. "What money are you talking about?"

"The money is in the shower, Millie."

"I thought you took that money to the bank long ago," the old woman called.

"No, Millie, not yet..."

"Well, why are they doing it? They're from where? How can they do this?"

"It's okay, honey," Davis reassured, as she approached the front door. "We're here to help you. Mr. Rivers saw this money in your house the other day, and we know it wasn't safe just lying around here. So we're going to put it in your bank account to make certain it's safe, and where they can keep track of it."

"What money? Kurt...help me..."

"It's okay, ma'am," Newell said stepping up to her. "They're just making sure the money's safe."

"But Kurt already took the money to the bank, months ago, didn't you, Kurt?"

Shrader did not answer her again. Instead he smoldered some more, cursing under his breath. "You can't do this!" he growled over and over again. "You can't do this."

"Go ahead, folks," Newell said. "Kurt, let's you and me get outside and simmer down."

"I'll come with you," Rives said. "We can talk some more about this."

Davis and Brennan followed the hallway to the back bedroom, as Sollie Rivers had directed them. They found the unused bathroom and the bone dry shower stall, inside of which rested the two sacks of cash.

Mildred kept wandering back to the bathroom. "What are you doing here?" she would call absent-mindedly. "Who are you?"

Mamie would lead her back to the living room, admonishing her to let the people do their jobs; until Mildred would break free again, and wander back to again question the intruders.

"Oh, my God..." Davis said, "...there's got to be $100,000 here, at least."

"At least, "Brennan said, "and look at this: most of the bills here are pretty worn and very old, as if decades old. But then there's a scattering of newer bills, as if they'd been placed her recently."

"Here, too," David said, running her hands through the bag.

"I wonder what this means," Brennan mused.

"I think most of the money has been here for a while, but someone's been stashing extra money in these bags as well."

"Shrader...y' think?"

"I wouldn't doubt it," she said. "Come on, let's take it to the bank. They can count it there."

Meanwhile, Kurt Shrader paced up and down the driveway in front, puffing on a cigarette, his face red and his eyes blazing. His reaction denoted a mixture of rage and panic. Officer Newell and Sollie Rivers watched him as he steamed. "You have no right to do this, no right! She's just an old woman!"

"We're just trying to do the right thing here," Rivers said. "We're just trying to protect her money..."

"Protect it from who...me?" Shrader shouted, getting up in River's face as he towered menacingly over him. "Is that what you're trying to say, you little...?

"C'mon Kurt," Newell urged, pulling Shrader back at the shoulder, "back off, Kurt...let's calm down!"

"Well, shit, Pete," Shrader raged, pacing up and down again. "He's practically accusing me of stealing from an old woman."

"Nobody's accusing anybody," Rivers said.

"C'mon, Kurt, you need to calm down," Newell asserted.

"I don't need to calm down!" Shrader barked, breaking away from his partner's grip.

Just then, Davis and Brennan emerged from the front door, carrying the two sacks of cash. "There's probably more than $100,000 here," Davis told Newell. "This definitely belongs in the bank."

"You knew about this?" Newell questioned Shrader, incredulously. "You're kidding!"

Shrader's face turned beat red, then suddenly he bolted.

"Screw you!" he shouted. Just as Brennan had feared, Shrader ran for the jeep, climbed in, screeched out of the driveway, and roared off. Newell stood stock still, astounded at what had just transpired. "I can't believe it," Newell exclaimed. "What the hell is he doing?"

"Where's he going?" Rivers said.

"I wonder if he's headed for the bank," Davis responded, "although I don't know what he'd do there."

"I don't know," Brennan replied. "He looked pretty desperate. He's likely t' try anything, whether it makes sense or not."

Newell pulled his cell phone from his belt, signaling the dispatcher. "What bank is it?"

"American Thrift," Rivers said, "at the edge of town."

Newell called in the incident to the disbelieving watch commander. Newell had three units sent to the bank, and one sent to pick him up. Davis, Rivers, and Brennan meanwhile climbed back into the Oldsmobile. They sped to American Thrift Bank, the court order in hand.

Customer service representative Tina McKay smiled as the next customer approached her teller's window at the bank. Tall, slender, with wavy brown hair in a business skirt and blouse, McKay smiled when she recognized the tall, muscular man with the gray mustache. She recalled the pleasant conversations they'd enjoyed in the past.

"Good morning, Mr. Shrader," she beamed as he approached her station. "Where is Millie today?"

Shrader shuffled, speaking quickly and sharply. "She's not feeling well", he said.

"Oh, I'm sorry to hear that," McKay said. "How can I help you?"

Shrader glanced tensely from side to side, and leaned closer toward the teller. "I would like to close out Millie's account," he said, holding forward the bank book.

"Excuse me?" McKay said, not sure what he'd told her.

Shrader clenched his teeth, and repeated more loudly, "We need to close out Millie's account!"

"Really…the whole thing…?" McKay inquired, startled at the prospect of losing a substantial account from a long time customer.

"Yes, the whole thing," Shrader stated.

"Since Millie wasn't able to come in today, were you able to obtain a statement in writing from her concerning this?"

"No…as I said, she's not feeling well."

"Well, I'm sorry, Mr. Shrader. Since your name is not on the account, I would need a written…"

"Please!" Shrader's bank echoed off the tile floor of the bank. His face twisted into a portrait of impending panic, as he slammed his open palm upon the counter. "I need to close that account now!"

McKay had never seen Kurt Shrader like this. Growing fearful, she looked around as if trying to attract the attention of fellow employees. "I'm sorry, Mr. Shrader…"

"I need that money…now!"

Shrader himself began to draw attention now, from both the employees and the customers of the bank. Some of the customers mumbled among themselves, and watched anxiously.

"Goddammit…" Shrader roared, "let me have that money!"

"Kurt", a deep male voice called from behind him. Shrader whirled and faced two uniformed Huntington police officers entering the bank from the north side. Two more officers entered through the south doors. "C'mon, Kurt", a stocky, black-haired officer called again, "it's time to go, buddy."

Shrader paused for a moment, but seemed to quickly resign himself to the hopelessness of the situation. He had been caught, and he knew it. "Damn…" he swore.

"C'mon, man," the officer called. "Let's go back to the station and talk about this. There's no reason to frighten that young woman, or anyone else in this bank."

Three officers by then had quietly surrounded Shrader at the teller's window, and led him toward the south bank door. The fourth policeman stayed to calm Tina McKay – who remained visibly shaken – and to take her statement concerning her unusual encounter with Kurt Shrader.

By the time the county car arrived at the bank, three police cars waited in the parking lot. As the APS workers approached the bank door, they found Kurt Shrader surrounded by Huntington Police officers. They led Shrader calmly to the back of one of the squad cars, just as Officer Newell arrived in a fourth car. He briefly conferred with the officers, and then came over to advise the social workers.

"Looks like he came to the bank to close down the account," Newell said. "Apparently he makes deposits and accompanies Mrs. Messanich for withdrawals a lot here. He approached one of the tellers he knew, but when the teller refused to close the account without Mrs. Messanich's authorization, he began shouting, demanding she close the account. That's when the units arrived. They came in and calmed him down, and now they're going to take him back to the precinct.

"Geeze," Rivers said.

"He was hiding cash in a grocery bag," Davis told him. "I bet he's been storing cash away from his various errands, and he's been keeping it in the bags of cash he found in the house. He knew she would never know the difference, and he knew as long as the money was in a sack in her house, the bank could neither track it nor freeze it. My guess is he was going to wait until she died, and then take all the money for himself, without a trace."

"Damn," said Newell, "he seemed like such a good cop to me."

"It sounds like he straddled the ethical fence so long, he eventually fell over the side," Brennan said. "The temptation was too great."

"I guess so," Newell agreed.

Newell agreed to accompany the APS workers until the money had been safely deposited. As counted by the teller, more than $149,000 had been stored in the bags. As predicted, most of the bills had been printed before 1960, but the last few thousand had emerged in the last decade.

Ari Davis finished the deposit, then handed Ms. McKay the court order to make a copy. Given the recent events, the teller seemed uncommonly willing to cooperate with the Deputy Public Guardian.

Over the next few weeks, Davis completed the petition for temporary and finally permanent conservatorship. Because of the wealth of assets, the court assigned a special fiduciary experienced in handling large estates. Mildred Messanich remained in her home with her housekeeper, never quite certain about who managed her money. She did notice Kurt Shrader did not come around anymore, but after a time not even that seemed to matter. Because of the size of the estate, the fiduciary was able to purchase all the help she would ever need, enabling her to remain in her home for the rest of her life.

Over the same few weeks details of Officer Kurt Shrader's plan to bilk money from the Messanich estate came to light. Under investigation by the District Attorney's office, Shrader revealed ever since Mildred's brother died, the officer started coming around the house to "help her." He soon discovered the stash of money hidden in the shower, a treasure apparently left by the brother. There had been no record where the cash had come from, and it soon became apparent to Shrader that Mildred had appa-rently forgotten all about it – if she ever even knew about it. No one else seemed to know about it either.

Resentful about the relatively meager salary he earned as a cop – particularly amid the wealth constantly surrounding him in Huntington – Shrader managed to convince himself of his entitlement to the money, in exchange for the services he rendered to Mildred. He also convinced himself she would never miss it.

Shrader, as a police officer, found it easy to earn Mildred's unquestioned trust. He soon became the woman's errand boy, and convinced her to write checks for groceries and good far beyond the amount needed. Sometimes he got her to write checks for "services rendered," always payable to "cash", to keep Shrader's name undocumented. Most of the change he would hide in the paper bags so – as Davis surmised – there would be no record of it, and the bank would not be able to keep track of it.

This went on for about five years, over which time Shrader managed to store more than $20,000 in addition to the original trove. He planned to eventually reach at least $150,000 in total, take one hundred grand for himself, and leave the rest in the bags. He would flee the country, and take up residence some where to live on the money. He figured there would be no record of the money, and he would get away free and clear. Obviously, he figured wrong.

The District Attorney adamantly condemned the lackadaisical practice of the Huntington Police Department with regard to the personal involvement in the day-to-day lives of the residents. The D.A. strictly encouraged Chief Fitzgerald to implement a policy change to control the possibility of this sort of thing happening again. Although Fitzgerald assured the reins would be tightened, the APS workers – having learning what they has about Huntington - wondered how many other arrangements were similar to Mildred and Shrader, and how much these entrenched practices would actually change.

The case drew considerable media attention – the last thing Chief Fitzgerald wanted - and certainly more than usually afforded an APS case. The enormous wealth involved in the case, the prominence of the Huntington community, and the illicit involvement of a police officer all invited inordinate public scrutiny. As usual, Marlene Gregg's office fielded the questions directed at Adult Services, to make certain responses would be issued in a uniform manner. Gregg hoped the media attention – as well as the district attorney's investigation- would help curb the unusual practices in the wealthy suburb of Huntington. She also hoped to shine a positive light on APS.

Sounds of laughter and celebration reverberated through the Big Room, as staff of Cedarwood County Adult Services – those not off on holiday leave – gathered on December 31 to usher in the New Year. A Christmas tree, draped in twinkling silver tinsel and brightly colored globes, decorated the office corner next to the copy machine. Garland, holiday cards, and festive illustrations covered the baffles and walls of the room. A punch bowl, brimming with a reddish-pink concoction, perched on the table outside the staff meeting room, flanked by an assortment of baked goodies and finger snack food. Everywhere social workers, nurses, supervisors, and clerks gathered in small enclaves, laughing and reveling in the celebrative atmosphere.

By some coincidence of fate – perhaps the alignment of the planets, the configuration of the stars, a mystical, unseen force – every member of Adult Protective Services staff occupied the Big Room at the same time. No one had requested time off for the holidays. Home visits and emergencies seemed to be placed on hold. No one called in sick.

Although some paperwork and phone calls had been completed, the unit spent most of the day wandering in and around the Bullpen, reminiscing in the situation and cases of the year, sharing the war stories affecting each of them most.

As the hours and minutes wore on, the unit ensemble found itself sitting in a circle in the Bullpen. They laughed and kidded among themselves, as they shared punch and cookies. This provided a rare opportunity for the staff to gather as teammates, outside the Thursday morning unit meeting, simply to enjoy each other's company.

As Emma Hayes, Bob Foster, and Donna Briar shared "Gladys stories" to the uproarious laughter of the other staff, Chuck Corley quietly entered the Bullpen, a glass of punch in his hand. He hovered about the unit's circle, finally half-sitting on the edge of Foster's desk. The supervisor sat back and watched the hilarity, a serene grin of satisfaction highlighting his face. Before long, the seven-member unit realized Chuck now sat among them. A moment of silence ensued, until Sollie Rivers – sitting in a chair next to Briar – piped up, "Hi, Chuck…what's up?"

"Nothing, really," Corley replied, as he suddenly became the focus of the gathering. "I saw you all over here, having a good time, so I decided to join you.

"Sure," Rivers spoke for the group, "come on it."

"Do you want a cookie?" Rhonda Pagan offered from River's right.

"Sure," Corley said, picking out an oatmeal with M&M's. "What are you all laughing about?"

"Oh…Gladys…" Hayes spoke up, "…we were sharing our encounters with her, and all the fun she's brought to our lives.

Everybody seemed to roll their eyes, and giggle at once.

"Oh, yes…" Corley echoed quietly, "…Gladys."

Silence filled the space again, as the supervisor's presence seemed to alter the dynamics of the interaction.

"Well," Corley said, "the Proclamation is up in my office, if you want to take a look at it."

Bewildered glances crossed the circle. "Proclamation…" Foster bellowed, "what proclamation?"

"You know, from the All-Staff meeting…the Board of Supervisors…Marlene…last month…?"

"Oh, yeah", Brennan said. "Our award…"

Foster stood up from his chair and peered over the cubicle wall into Chuck's office. "Now, that's impressive," he said. He saw a laminated plaque with the Old English font letters spelling "Proclamation," although he could barely discern the other words, the except for the phrase, "The Do Something Crew", in bold italic letters.

"Has this become out nickname suddenly?" Foster griped.

"What's that?" asked Pagan.

Oh…you know…The Do Something Crew."

"Oh, yeah," Brennan said, "that's you're idea, eh Chuck?"

"Yes, actually," he answered. "I thought it was appropriate, with all the calls we get from the community for you to "do something!"

"Yeah, I guess," Rivers said. "Half the time they don't even know what they want us to do…just do something…"

"That's right," Briar agreed, as the rest of the circle nodded.

"Well, I think it's appropriate," Ari Davis said. "We're willing and able to actually do something, unlike a lot of other agencies."

"Yeah, and actually…" Foster added, "…a lot of times it don't matter what we do…as long as we respond, somehow…"

"But we have the flexibility and the leeway to do – or at least try – a lot of different things," Rivers said. "That's a tribute to you, Chuck."

"Thank you, Sollie," Corley said. "I think it's a tribute to all of you, too. You are willing to do something, to take risks, to go into unique situations and engage very unique characters, and struggle to come up with solutions to these problems. I find every work day to be a fascinating one, one that challenges me both as a professional and as a human being."

"I agree," said Hayes. "I know a lot of people working in this field, who are in job settings much more stressful than this one. This work is hard enough, but if we had to work in an environment just as difficult, it would be intolerable."

"Well, again," Corley added, "I heartily commend all of you. I am constantly amazed at the extent to which you all are willing to reach out to each other for consultation, for information, for support. It's rare, and in truth, my role of supervisor is made much easier because you are willing to help each other. That doesn't happen everywhere," he said."

"Aw…garsh," Rivers said.

"I feel a group hug coming on," Hayes quipped.

Everyone snickered.

"Seriously," Chuck said. "One of the reasons I came over here – since I amazingly found you all in one spot at the same time – is simply to thank you for an amazing year, and for creating such an amazing place to work."

Chuck raised his cup and toasted each member of the unit: "To Bob…Ari…Rhonda…Donna…Sollie…Emma…and Patrick: the Do Something Crew!"

"The Do Something Crew" the unit toasted collectively.

They stood in silence, enjoying the warmth and camaraderie of the moment. Suddenly, the Hotline bell rang. The moment ended.

Donna Briar reached over to her desk, lifted the receiver, and answered:

"Cedarwood Adult Services…can I help you?"

9006292R0

Made in the USA
Charleston, SC
02 August 2011